Reducing Quantities Chart

Sometimes the most effective technique for reducing fat and calories while maintaining flavor is to simply reduce the amount, which can have a significant impact.

Instead of	Reduce the amount to	Calories saved	Fat saved (grams)
1 cup chopped almonds	¾ cup	192	17
	⅔ cup	257	23
	½ cup	385	34
	⅓ cup	516	45
	¼ cup	578	51
1 cup shredded coconut	¾ cup	116	8
	⅔ cup	156	11
	½ cup	233	17
	⅓ cup	311	22
	¼ cup	350	25
1 cup chopped hazelnuts	¾ cup	182	21
	⅔ cup	243	24
	½ cup	364	36
	⅓ cup	485	48
	¼ cup	545	54
1 cup chopped pecans	¾ cup	198	20
	⅔ cup	265	27
	½ cup	397	40
	⅓ cup	530	54
	¼ cup	596	60
1 cup chopped walnuts	¾ cup	192	19
	⅔ cup	257	25
	½ cup	385	37
	⅓ cup	516	50
	¼ cup	578	56

Instead of	Reduce the amount to	Calories saved	Fat saved (grams)
1 cup chocolate chips	¾ cup	215	15
	⅔ cup	287	20
	½ cup	430	30
	⅓ cup	574	41
	¼ cup	645	46
1 cup peanut butter	¾ cup	379	32
	⅔ cup	507	43
	½ cup	758	64
	⅓ cup	1012	86
	¼ cup	1138	97
1 cup peanut butter chips	¾ cup	320	16
	⅔ cup	428	21
	½ cup	640	32
	⅓ cup	858	43
	¼ cup	960	48
1 cup white sugar*	¾ cup	192	0
	⅔ cup	256	0
	½ cup	385	0
	⅓ cup	513	0
	¼ cup	578	0

*In most recipes, you can reduce the amount of sugar by one-fourth to one-third. You can enhance sweetness by adding sweet spices and extracts such as cinnamon or vanilla. In drop cookies, the sugar melts and makes the cookies spread out, so you will have to substitute more liquid.

Healthy
Homestyle
Desserts

Other Books by Evelyn Tribole

Intuitive Eating (coauthor)
Healthy Homestyle Cooking
Eating on the Run, *second edition*

Healthy

❧❧❧❧❧

Homestyle

❧❧❧❧❧

Desserts

*150 Fabulous Treats
with a Fraction
of the Fat and Calories*

Evelyn Tribole, M.S., R.D.

Photographs by Sally Ann Ullman

VIKING

VIKING
Published by the Penguin Group
Penguin Books USA Inc., 375 Hudson Street,
New York, New York 10014, U.S.A.
Penguin Books Ltd, 27 Wrights Lane,
London W8 5TZ, England
Penguin Books Australia Ltd, Ringwood,
Victoria, Australia
Penguin Books Canada Ltd, 10 Alcorn Avenue,
Toronto, Ontario, Canada M4V 3B2
Penguin Books (N.Z.) Ltd, 182–190 Wairau Road,
Auckland 10, New Zealand

Penguin Books Ltd, Registered Offices:
Harmondsworth, Middlesex, England

First published in 1996 by Viking Penguin,
a division of Penguin Books USA Inc.

10 9 8 7 6 5 4 3 2 1

LIBRARY OF CONGRESS CATALOGING IN PUBLICATION DATA

Tribole, Evelyn, 1959–
    Healthy homestyle desserts / Evelyn Tribole.
        p.   cm.
    Includes index.
    ISBN 0-670-86626-1 (alk. paper)
    1. Desserts.   2. Low-fat diet—Recipes.   3. Low-calorie diet—
Recipes.   I. Title.
    TX773.T75   1996
    641.8'6—dc20   96-14105

This book is printed on acid-free paper.

∞

Printed in the United States of America
Set in Weiss
Designed by Richard Oriolo / Composed by Joseph Eagle, Maryland Linotype

To Connor,
who at age eighteen months
delighted in repeating a
new word, "tiramisù," over
and over again.
May you always know
the pleasure of eating and
good health.

Contents

Foreword

As a professional specializing in physical fitness and healthful living, I value the importance of creating a balanced program of regular exercise and nutritious eating. I have personally found that combining good foods and fun physical activities is fundamental to staying healthy and happy.

With the right mix, we can eat a wide variety of foods that meet our nutritional needs and satisfy our emotional wants. I believe strongly in some healthful guiding principles: 1. Do not deprive yourself; 2. Understand your sweet tooth; 3. If you like desserts for their soothing qualities, make them healthful most of the time; 4. Eat regularly throughout the day for a more balanced appetite; 5. Enjoy your body.

One way to eat well is to limit fat content in our diet. In an extension of her popular "Recipe Makeover" column that appears regularly in *Shape* magazine, Evelyn Tribole, M.S., R.D., has compiled easy-to-follow recipes that are packed with useful tidbits on fat-cutting techniques. Her nutrition scorecard lets you know how each recipe fits into your calorie and fat-intake goals.

And best of all, Evelyn does not compromise in the taste department. You'll be satisfied and delighted with the recipes. Share them with your friends.

So top off your next meal with a healthy homestyle dessert and get the best of both worlds—please your taste buds and meet your nutritional goals.

A cookie lover for as long as I can remember, I can't wait to enjoy Evelyn's incredible recipes. So indulge yourself, and your taste buds.

Barbara S. Harris
Editor in chief
Shape magazine

Acknowledgments

Y ou never *really* know how a dessert will turn out until you make and taste it. I am grateful to all my friends, family, and neighbors who after tasting the fifteenth cheesecake, the twentieth cookie, and so on . . . agreed to give their candid opinions at a moment's notice. Once I received the thumbs-up from them, it was on to the "official recipe testing."

I am especially indebted to Lari Robling, professional recipe tester, who cheerfully tested all my creations. I met Lari at QVC, where she prepped and styled all my food segments. I was so impressed with her work I asked if she'd be my recipe tester, and it was one of my best decisions. Lari's creative talents also shone as part of the food photography team, which also included Linda Carr as prop and background stylist. Thanks to Sally Ann Ullman, who took the gorgeous photographs themselves.

Special thanks to:

Dawn Drzal, a terrific editor and enthusiastic supporter, who often went beyond the call of duty to get the job done right. She took buses to the country, put me up in her apartment for a couple of nights, and upon learning that I love French caramels, managed to bring a few pieces across the Atlantic from her trip to France. That is a dedicated and thoughtful editor.

David Smith, my literary agent and all-around good guy. I am lucky to have such a caring and ardent agent.

Book publicists past (and future). These are important people to a book, because they help get the word out. Yet by the time you meet them it's after the book is in print and they never get a proper thank you. Special thanks to Mary Lengle, Linda Johns, and Nicholas Scibbeta, publicists from past books.

Most important, thank you to my family for their patience, love, and understanding.

Acknowledgments

Introduction

⚮ ⚮ ⚮

Ahhh, dessert. Whether on a television show or in a workshop, I found it's easy to convince people that healthful eating doesn't have to be blah by having them taste low-fat desserts. It's the old you-catch-more-flies-with-honey technique. Usually, I wait for satisfied grins to appear, and then announce the healthful ingredient change or secret surprise—such as using baby-food prunes in place of butter. Tasting is believing, and it often motivates people. They think, "Gee, if a dessert is this good, how can I experiment with my other recipes?"

While I have found desserts to be a good springboard into healthy eating, the truth is I simply love desserts. (I was once tracked down by a reporter because she heard that I was "the dietitian that loves to eat desserts.") But how do you include dessert in a healthy eating style? Even low-fat desserts have their share of calories, sugar, and fat. In fact, if you looked into my shopping cart while I was preparing this book, at first glance you'd be surprised that I am a nutritionist.

But the reality is that while there is no nutritional need for chocolate or cheesecake, most health-conscious people still crave a satisfying dessert they can sink their teeth into. The good news is that desserts and health are not mutually exclusive—you *can* have your dessert and health, too! It's the dose that makes the poison or the cure. One food, one meal, one day will not make or break your health. It's how much you eat consistently over time.

Even the tip of the USDA's Food Pyramid allows room for some goodies. Fortunately, all the recipes in this book are significantly reduced in both calories and fat. (In fact there are a hundred recipes that have 5 grams or less of fat, and over ninety recipes under 250 calories.)

How to Make the Most of Desserts

Having a healthy relationship with food is just as important as what you eat. I find that many of us need an adjustment in our attitude toward food, because eating has become such a moral issue in this country—and unhealthy food a sinful indulgence. Desserts, especially, have been vilified. Let's first look at how to get a healthy food attitude. Then I'll explain how to make a dessert more healthy by tinkering with the ingredients.

Look for Satisfaction

One of the reasons I decided to create a healthy dessert cookbook was that I was so tired of "air food" desserts, where all the fun and satisfaction was taken out with the calories. I truly believe that if you are left unsatisfied, you will be on the prowl for more food. For example, in many cases I would much rather have *real* chocolate chips in a chocolate chip cookie (perhaps just fewer) than substitute with carob chips or raisins. Pleeeease! Carob is not chocolate. Raisins are not chocolate. And if you try hitting your "chocolate spot" with something other than chocolate, you are likely to end up eating many more calories in the long run. I once had a client who was really craving a chocolate chip cookie. She tried to fend if off by eating vanilla wafers. After about ten vanilla wafers, she realized that they were not hitting the spot, and so she ate the chocolate chip cookie anyway. Now she had the chocolate chip calories *plus* the vanilla wafer calories!

Savor the Dessert Experience

If a dessert is worth eating, then be sure to make eating it a worthwhile experience. Otherwise, you may find yourself going back for seconds in search of the missed food experience. Also, if you don't love it, don't eat it.

Say Good-bye to Guilt and Forbidden Foods

Desserts have often been exiled to the world of forbidden foods. Consequently, if you view dessert as a giant no-no, the guilt that ensues after indulging can easily lead to overeating. A study published in the *American Journal of Clinical Nutrition* found that people who successfully maintained their weight did not forbid themselves any food they truly enjoyed. While they tended to eat less fat and sugar, they made efforts to avoid feeling deprived by allowing themselves some favorite foods.

Be Careful of the Fat-Free Trap

It's all too easy to get caught up into the it's-fat-free-so-I-can-eat-as-much-as-I-want trap. Big problem. Fat-free is not calorie-free (even in my recipes). And once you overeat, as far as the body is concerned, calories are calories regardless of their source. Excess calories *will* turn into fat. No matter how healthy a food is, it's still important to listen to your body and honor its satiety signals.

Food Philosophy: Ingredients Make a Difference

Taste is just as important as nutrition. If something doesn't taste very good, you are not likely to eat it. In the case of desserts, it might mean going back to the full-fat version. Taste is so important to me that each of the recipes in this book was tested at least twice. If a recipe I created passed my standards *and* the taste buds of my testers, it went on for round two of testing by an independent professional recipe tester.

While trying to balance taste and nutrition, I strive for the following goals when making over a recipe:

- Reduce the fat and calories (without compromising taste).

- Use healthier ingredients (such as whole-wheat flour instead of all-purpose flour when possible).

- Reduce the salt, usually by half or more.

Fat- and Calorie-Saving Techniques

I have highlighted the fat-cutting and calorie-cutting procedures in each recipe. By doing so, I hope to pass on the techniques so that you can cut the fat in your favorite recipes. There are many ways to carve away the fat and calories, but the techniques usually fall into one of three categories:

- Replace a high-fat ingredient with one that's lower in fat and calories (such as using applesauce instead of oil in a muffin).

- Reduce the quantity of the fatty ingredient or eliminate it altogether (such as reducing the amount of nuts in a bread).

- Use a low-fat cooking method (such as baking doughnuts instead of frying).

I've compiled two charts that clearly show how either substituting an ingredient or simply reducing the quantity can have an impact on calories and fat (see the charts on the endpapers).

Here are a few of my favorite ingredient tricks with a few tips on when and how to use them in a dessert recipe.

Evaporated skim milk It makes a great substitute for cream in recipes such as puddings and pumpkin pie. While the skim milk has no significant fat, the dense liquid helps to give a full-bodied consistency. It can also be whipped.

Buttermilk I am fond using buttermilk for the liquid ingredient in low-fat baking—especially cakes, muffins, and brownies. While the name *buttermilk* may conjure up images of a fatty liquid, the fat content is actually comparable to the amount of fat found in low-fat milk. Using buttermilk helps get rid of the rubbery texture that tends to result from fat-free baking.

Eggs Anytime a recipe calls for eggs, you can usually substitute two egg whites for each whole egg. Egg whites are naturally fat-free and have no cholesterol. Because of their high protein content, I usually like to beat them until foamy when using them in baked products such as cakes. This helps to create a more tender product.

Phyllo dough A very easy substitute for puff pastry and even pie crust. The trick is to use nonstick vegetable spray instead of butter. Don't be intimidated by the paper-thin texture. While phyllo sheets tend to dry out and crack, this problem is very easy to overcome by covering the unused sheets with a damp cloth. Keep in mind that the ample amount of sheets found in one box allow for a lot of experimentation and edible mistakes!

Nuts Nuts are one ingredient that is noticeably absent if omitted. Generally, it's very easy to reduce the amount of nuts by one-fourth to one-half. I will often chop nuts into fine pieces to help distribute the flavor. If texture is one of the main reasons nuts are used in a recipe, try adding other crunchy textures, such as a crisp rice cereal or nugget-type cereal. This works particularly well in nonbaked goods such as ice cream toppings.

Cocoa powder Cocoa is much lower in fat than baking chocolate. Generally, you can replace all or part of the baking chocolate with cocoa powder, depending on the recipe and desired texture. For example, if you desire a fudgy-type brownie, replace only half the baking chocolate with cocoa powder. If, however, you prefer cakelike brownies, you can replace all the chocolate with cocoa powder.

Mini chocolate chips When a recipe calls for chocolate chips, I usually use the mini chips—they go a lot farther. You can usually reduce the amount of chips by half.

Fruit purees (applesauce and prune) I am a fan of using fruit purees instead of butter or oil in baked goods. I generally use baby-food prunes in recipes containing chocolate and unsweetened applesauce for the others. A special note about prune puree: I prefer using the baby-food prunes because they're ready to use—there's no cooking or cleaning up a gummed-up food processor. They also have a more subtle flavor than prunes that are pureed from scratch.

Vanilla pudding mix When made with nonfat milk in a reduced quantity (from one-third to one-half of the usual amount for a pudding), it makes an easy filling that's also fat-free. (Check out the Boston Cream Pie on page 176.)

Special Mention of Fat–Free Foods

While I am thrilled that there is a host of new reduced-fat ingredients, keep in mind that they usually do not possess the same baking characteristics as their original counterparts. Sometimes a fat-free counterpart is clearly inferior in a recipe, so I will use a higher-fat product instead. Keep in mind these tips when using new reduced-fat foods:

- Don't assume that you can automatically substitute a fat-free counterpart and get the same results. They are often made with extra water or other ingredients, such as gelatin, that will break down when heated.

- Be familiar with how the product tastes before you add it to a recipe. There can be a remarkable taste and texture difference from brand to brand.

Here are some of the newer crop of reduced-fat foods, and some tips for working with them.

Light butter Light butter has half the fat of real butter and tastes sensational. Most of the fat is replaced by water, however. That extra water content makes a big difference in baking, especially in cookies. I usually compensate by using less liquid and sometimes omitting an egg white.

Fat-free sour cream This product works remarkably well in recipes. Be sure to choose a brand without gelatin for the best results. Or choose a brand in which gelatin is listed lowest in the ingredients.

Low-fat "baking chips" This substitute for chocolate chips was recently introduced by Hershey. These chips are made lower in fat by using a fat replacer, Salatrim. Salatrim is made from the same acids found in vinegar, cheese, and vegetable oil but has about half the calories of fat (5 calories rather than 9 calories per gram). I did my own side-by-side unscientific taste test (in the interest of health, of course) and found the texture of these test-tube morsels to be gritty and not quite as chocolaty as the regular chips. I might be willing to put up with these attributes if there were a greater nutrition payoff. While the reduced-fat chips have 50 percent less fat, they are only 10 calories less compared with regular (60 versus 70 per tablespoon). And there is *more* sugar in the reduced-fat chips than in the regular.

Fat-free cream cheese Fat-free cream cheese has come a long way since it first appeared in the dairy case. It can now work remarkably well in cheesecake, although I prefer to mix it with a combination of light cream cheese and pureed nonfat cottage cheese for a winning flavor and texture combination. There is a problem, however. When you combine the fat-free cream cheese with liquid ingredients, tiny lumps form, resembling cottage cheese curds. This can be overcome by softening the fat-free cream cheese at room temperature and then mixing it with light cream cheese. The fat in the light cream cheese helps serve as an emulsifier and prevents the clumping.

Fat-free loaf cakes No problem here. These come in marble, golden, or chocolate and work very well in trifle, tiramisù, and anywhere else that you might use regular pound cake or lady fingers. Just remember, however, that an entire cake averages about 1,000 calories.

Fat-free caramel and fudge sauces These taste surprisingly good and require no modifications when served over ice cream or other desserts.

Now, armed with these guidelines and the recipes that follow, you can serve healthier homestyle desserts to your family and guests. Happy guilt-free eating!

Flavor Savors

To enhance the flavor of your favorite desserts or to add a little more richness, try some of these ideas:

✒ Toast nuts to bring out their nutty aromatic flavor. Just scatter them on a baking sheet in a 350° F. oven and bake until light brown and an aroma resembling popcorn is produced, about 10 minutes. If I'm in a real hurry, I'll just shove them under the broiler—but this takes a watchful eye, because they can easily burn. Broiling takes about 2 to 3 minutes.

✒ Flavor extracts such as coconut and mint can really perk up a recipe. It's much easier to reduce or eliminate flaked coconut when you incorporate the rich tropical flavor of coconut extract.

✒ Finishing off a dessert sauce with just a hint of butter can add a tremendous amount of richness and flavor.

✒ Adding ½ to 1 teaspoon instant coffee granules to a chocolate dessert helps to intensify the chocolate flavor.

✒ Add sweet spices such as cinnamon, nutmeg, or cardamom to enhance the perception of sweetness.

✒ Split a vanilla bean, scrape out the seeds, and add them to your favorite vanilla desserts, such as vanilla pudding or custard. While vanilla beans are expensive, you haven't tasted vanilla until you've used one of these in a recipe.

❋ ❋ ❋ ❋ ❋

Common Problems: Troubleshooting Guide

Topic	Problem	Tips
Cakes	Tough texture	1. Beat egg whites until opaque in color and soft peak form. 2. Try using buttermilk as the prime liquid. It adds body and softens up the texture.
Cheesecake	Lumpy batter	1. Be sure that cream cheese is softened completely at room temperature. 2. If light cream cheese is in the recipe, be sure to mix with fat-free cream cheese before adding any other ingredients. 3. If cottage cheese is being used, be sure it's pureed until smooth and resembles fluffy marshmallow creme. If you have a weak food processor or a blender, try pushing the cottage cheese through a fine sieve with the back of a spoon, then puree.
Cheesecake	Excessive cracking during baking or cooling	1. Be sure not to overbeat after adding egg whites. (This is one time you do not want to beat the egg whites until foamy.) 2. Just before pouring batter into the springform pan, try tapping the bowl containing the batter on the countertop. This helps break up trapped air. 3. Try letting the cheesecake batter stand in the springform pan for about 20 minutes before baking—this allows the air to settle.
Cookies	Rubbery	1. Eliminate an egg white. 2. Be sure to let them cool on a wire rack. Otherwise the moisture released from the steam gets trapped (it's like giving your cookies a steam bath).
Egg whites	Won't thicken or stiffen up when beating	1. Be sure you are using egg whites or egg white powder. Egg sub-stitutes will not beat into a stiff peak and are not suitable for meringues. 2. Make sure you are using a clean bowl and beaters. Just a speck of fat will inhibit the egg whites from increasing their volume.
Muffins and breads	Too wet	1. If recipe uses fat-free sour cream, be sure it has no gelatin, or gelatin is listed toward the bottom of the ingredient list. 2. Substituting white flour for whole-wheat can cause this problem. If a recipe calls for whole-wheat flour, be sure to use it. Whole-wheat flour absorbs liquid because of its high fiber content.
Muffins and breads	Too tough or rubbery texture	1. Beat egg whites until foamy. 2. Add a grated apple or moist vegetable such as carrot or zucchini.

Gooey and

✣ ✣ ✣ ✣ ✣

Chewy Bars

✣ ✣ ✣ ✣ ✣

and

✣ ✣ ✣ ✣ ✣

Brownies

Five-Layer Bars

Makes 36 bars

✄ ✄ ✄ ✄

These inviting treats are so easy to make! My family couldn't believe that these were the low-fat *version of the popular cookie bar.*

How fat and calories were lowered:

- ☞ Replaced a stick of margarine with a combination of jam and an egg white to bind the bottom layer

- ☞ Replaced part of the graham crackers with a nugget cereal

- ☞ Used fewer chocolate chips, coconut, and pecans

- ☞ Substituted low-fat sweetened condensed milk for the regular version

Nutrition Scorecard
(per bar)

	Before	After
Calories	208	133
Fat (grams)	13	5
% calories from fat	54	32
Cholesterol (mg)	18	2

1 cup graham cracker crumbs

½ cup nugget cereal (such as Grape-Nuts)

4 tablespoons fruit-only apricot jam

1 egg white

1 (14-ounce) can low-fat sweetened
   condensed milk

½ cup semisweet chocolate chips

¾ cup flaked coconut

½ cup chopped pecans

Preheat the oven to 350° F. Lightly coat a 13x9-inch baking pan with nonstick vegetable-oil spray. In a large bowl, combine the graham cracker crumbs and nugget cereal; set aside. In a small microwavable cup, warm the jam in the microwave on High (about 10 seconds). Combine the egg white and jam; using a fork, stir into the crumb mixture. Press the mixture into the prepared pan. Pour the low-fat sweetened condensed milk evenly over the crumb layer. Sprinkle the remaining ingredients evenly over the top. Bake 25 to 30 minutes, or until lightly browned. Let cool, in the pan, on a wire rack. Chill if desired. Cut into bars.

Apricot Oat Bars

Makes 36 bars

❈ ❈ ❈ ❈ ❈

*T*his is an easy treat to make—what's hard is eating just one of these delectable bars.

How fat and calories were lowered:

☛ Replaced butter with a combination of buttermilk, oil, and walnuts

☛ Used less coconut

Nutrition Scorecard
(per bar)

	Before	After
Calories	94	73
Fat (grams)	4	2
% calories from fat	42	23
Cholesterol (mg)	10	<1

Bars

1 ¼ cups quick oats

1 ¼ cups all-purpose flour

½ cup sugar

⅓ cup walnuts

½ teaspoon finely grated lemon zest

½ teaspoon baking soda

⅛ teaspoon salt

½ cup buttermilk

2 tablespoons oil

Topping

1 (10-ounce) jar fruit-only apricot preserves

1 tablespoon old-fashioned oats

⅓ cup flaked coconut

Preheat the oven to 350° F. Lightly coat a 13x9-inch baking pan with nonstick vegetable-oil spray. In a large bowl, combine the oats, flour, sugar, walnuts, lemon zest, baking soda, and salt. Add the buttermilk and oil. Beat at low speed, scraping the bowl often. Press the dough into the prepared pan.

For topping, spread the preserves evenly over the dough. Sprinkle with the 1 tablespoon oats and top with the coconut. Bake for 20 to 25 minutes, or until the edges are lightly browned. Let cool completely, in the pan, on a wire rack. Cut into small bars.

Macaroon Brownies

Makes 20 brownies

ᕽ ᕽ ᕽ ᕽ

Hands down, these are my favorite brownies—and they look so irresistible, too. You'll be proud to serve these to company.

How fat and calories were lowered:

- ☞ Used less nuts and coconut
- ☞ Substituted baby-food prunes for butter
- ☞ Replaced baking chocolate with a combination of cocoa powder and mini chocolate chips
- ☞ Used egg whites in place of whole eggs
- ☞ Used fat-free cream cheese in place of regular cream cheese

Nutrition Scorecard
(per brownie)

	Before	After
Calories	216	136
Fat (grams)	13	4
% calories from fat	53	25
Cholesterol (mg)	40	1

Macaroon Topping

4 ounces fat-free cream cheese

⅓ cup sugar

1 egg white

4 teaspoons all-purpose flour

½ teaspoon coconut extract

¾ cup flaked coconut

Brownies

¼ cup whole-wheat flour

½ cup all-purpose flour

1 cup sugar

½ cup unsweetened cocoa powder

½ teaspoon baking powder

4 egg whites

1 (2½-ounce) jar baby-food prunes

⅓ cup buttermilk

1 teaspoon vanilla extract

½ cup mini chocolate chips

¼ cup toasted chopped almonds

Chocolate Drizzle

1 tablespoon mini chocolate chips, melted

Preheat the oven to 350° F. Lightly coat an 8x8-inch baking pan with nonstick vegetable-oil spray.

To make the macaroon topping: Mix the cream cheese, sugar, egg white, flour, and coconut extract until smooth. Stir in the flaked coconut. Set aside.

To make the brownies: In a large bowl, combine the whole-wheat flour, all-purpose flour, sugar, cocoa powder, and baking powder.

In a medium bowl, beat the egg whites until foamy; add the baby-food prunes, buttermilk, and vanilla. Add the egg white mixture to the flour mixture and mix until blended. Stir in the chocolate chips and almonds. Spread the batter in the prepared baking pan.

Spread the macaroon topping over the brownie batter. Bake 25 to 30 minutes. Let cool, in the pan, on a wire rack. Drizzle with the melted chocolate chips. (Decorative tip: Swirl a toothpick through the melted chips after drizzling them on the brownies.)

Whole-Wheat vs. All-Purpose Flour

It makes sense to incorporate whole-wheat flour into your recipes when possible. Consider the nutritional power of whole-wheat flour compared to white flour. Whole-Wheat flour has:

- Six times more magnesium

- Five times more fiber

- Four times more potassium

- Three times (nearly) the selenium content

- Twice the vitamin E content

Pumpkin Bars

Makes 48 bars

❈❈ ❈❈ ❈❈

These cakelike bars are an absolute winner. The light cream cheese frosting accents the pumpkin flavor for a delectable treat. I used whole-wheat flour to boost the nutrition.

How fat and calories were lowered:

☞ Replaced oil with a combination of buttermilk and unsweetened applesauce

☞ Used egg whites instead of whole eggs

☞ Reduced amount of sugar

☞ Used marshmallow creme in place of butter in the frosting

Nutrition Scorecard *(per bar)*		
	Before	After
Calories	159	75
Fat (grams)	8	1
% calories from fat	46	11
Cholesterol (mg)	27	2

Pumpkin Bars

1 cup all-purpose flour

1 cup whole-wheat flour

1¼ cups sugar

2 teaspoons baking powder

2 teaspoons cinnamon

1 teaspoon baking soda

¼ teaspoon ground cloves

6 egg whites, beaten until foamy

1 (16-ounce) can pumpkin

½ cup buttermilk

½ cup unsweetened applesauce

Cream Cheese Frosting

1 (7½-ounce) jar marshmallow creme

8 ounces tub-style light cream cheese
  (not fat-free)

1 teaspoon fresh lemon juice

1 teaspoon vanilla extract

¾ cup powdered sugar

Preheat the oven to 350° F. Lightly coat a 15x10x1-inch baking pan with nonstick vegetable-oil spray. In a large bowl, combine the all-purpose flour, whole-wheat flour, sugar, baking powder, cinnamon, baking soda, and cloves. Stir in the egg whites, pumpkin, buttermilk, and applesauce until thoroughly combined. Spread the batter into the prepared pan.

Bake for 25 to 30 minutes, or until a toothpick inserted near the center comes out clean. Let cool, in the pan, on a wire rack.

To make the frosting: In a medium bowl, beat together the marshmallow creme, light cream cheese, lemon juice, and vanilla until light and fluffy. Gradually add the powdered sugar, beating well.

Frost the bars with the cream cheese frosting.

Orange Date Bars

Makes 20 bars

ʒ⋉ ʒ⋉ ʒ⋉ ʒ⋉ ʒ⋉

The zing of citrus enlivens these delicious bars. This tasty treat makes a great afternoon snack or treat for the lunch box.

How fat and calories were lowered:

☞ Used applesauce instead of butter

☞ Reduced the amount of nuts

☞ Replaced the whole egg with egg whites

Nutrition Scorecard
(per bar)

	Before	After
Calories	104	75
Fat (grams)	4	1
% calories from fat	37	15
Cholesterol (mg)	17	0

½ cup all-purpose flour

½ cup whole-wheat flour

½ cup packed light brown sugar

1 teaspoon grated orange zest

½ teaspoon baking powder

¼ teaspoon baking soda

½ cup fresh orange juice

¼ cup unsweetened applesauce

2 egg whites, beaten until foamy

½ cup chopped pitted dates

⅓ cup chopped walnuts, toasted

1 tablespoon powdered sugar, for sifting
    over top

Preheat the oven to 350° F. Lightly coat an 11x7x1½-inch baking pan with nonstick vegetable-oil spray. In a large mixing bowl, combine the all-purpose flour, whole-wheat flour, brown sugar, orange zest, baking powder, and baking soda. Add the orange juice, applesauce, and beaten egg whites. Beat until thoroughly combined. Stir in the dates and walnuts.

Spread the batter into the prepared pan. Bake about 25 minutes, or until a toothpick inserted near the center comes out clean. Let cool, in the pan, on a wire rack. Sift the powdered sugar over the top. Cut into bars.

Black Forest Brownies

Makes 16 large brownies

✉ ✉ ✉ ✉ ✉

So simple to make! This fancy three-layer dessert gets a head start by using a commercial brownie mix.

How fat and calories were lowered:

☞ Replaced whipping cream with a combination of nonfat milk and sugar-free pudding

☞ Used egg whites and baby-food prunes in brownies

☞ Reduced the amount of semisweet chocolate

☞ Used reduced-fat cream cheese instead of regular cream cheese

Nutrition Scorecard
(per brownie)

	Before	After
Calories	418	260
Fat (grams)	18	6
% calories from fat	41	23
Cholesterol (mg)	36	6

2 egg whites

2 (2½-ounce) jars baby-food prunes

½ cup buttermilk

1 (21½-ounce) package regular brownie mix (13x9-inch pan size)

1 1-ounce package sugar-free instant vanilla pudding

1½ cups nonfat milk

8 ounces tub-style light cream cheese, softened at room temperature

2 20-ounce cans light cherry pie filling

1-ounce square semisweet chocolate, melted

Preheat the oven to 350° F. Lightly coat a 13x9x2-inch baking pan with nonstick vegetable-oil spray. In a large bowl, mix together the egg whites, baby-food prunes, and buttermilk until blended. Stir in the brownie mix well. Spread batter in prepared pan. Bake for 30 to 35 minutes. Let cool, in the pan, on a wire rack.

In a medium bowl, combine the pudding and nonfat milk; beat on low to mix. Add the light cream cheese and beat until smooth and thickened. Spread over the cooled brownie layer. Top with the cherry pie filling. Chill 30 minutes, or until the cheese topping is firm. Cut into squares. Using the tines of a fork, drizzle melted chocolate over each square.

Healthy Homestyle Desserts

Peanut Butter Chip Brownies

Makes 30 brownies

✂ ✂ ✂ ✂

For you peanut butter chocolate lovers this brownie is an absolute winner.

How fat and calories were lowered:

✎ Used baby-food prunes and buttermilk in place of oil

✎ Used less peanut butter chips and sugar

✎ Used egg whites instead of whole eggs

Nutrition Scorecard (per brownie)	Before	After
Calories	175	114
Fat (grams)	8	3
% calories from fat	43	20
Cholesterol (mg)	14	0

4 egg whites

½ cup buttermilk

1 (2½-ounce) jar baby-food prunes

1 teaspoon vanilla extract

¾ cup unsweetened cocoa powder

½ teaspoon baking soda

½ cup boiling water

1¾ cups sugar

1 cup all-purpose flour

⅓ cup whole-wheat flour

1¼ cups peanut butter chips

Preheat the oven to 350° F. Lightly coat a 13x9-inch baking pan with nonstick vegetable-oil spray. In a medium bowl, beat the egg whites until foamy; stir in the buttermilk, baby-food prunes, and vanilla; set aside. In a large bowl, combine the cocoa and baking soda. Add the boiling water and stir until mixture thickens. Add the egg white mixture and stir until smooth. Add the sugar, all-purpose flour, and whole-wheat flour; blend completely. Stir in the peanut butter chips. Bake for 25 to 30 minutes, or until a toothpick inserted near the center comes out clean. Let cool, in the pan, on a wire rack.

Chocolate and Magnesium

One-fourth cup of cocoa powder provides 104 milligrams of magnesium, or about 25 percent of your daily needs.

✂ ✂ ✂ ✂

Double Chocolate Chip Brownies

Makes 20 brownies

✄ ✄ ✄ ✄ ✄

*I*t's hard to believe that these moist, chocolaty brownies are made primarily from whole-wheat flour. The mini chocolate chips make this treat especially satisfying.

How fat and calories were lowered:

☞ Replaced baking chocolate with unsweetened cocoa powder

☞ Used baby-food prunes instead of butter

☞ Reduced the amount of nuts

☞ Used fewer chocolate chips and used a smaller size

Nutrition Scorecard *(per brownie)*		
	Before	*After*
Calories	194	112
Fat (grams)	12.5	4
% calories from fat	54	29

½ cup whole-wheat flour

¼ cup all-purpose flour

1 cup sugar

½ cup unsweetened cocoa powder

½ teaspoon baking powder

4 egg whites

1 (2½-ounce) jar baby-food prunes

⅓ cup buttermilk

2 teaspoons vanilla extract

⅔ cup mini chocolate chips

⅓ cup chopped walnuts

Preheat the oven to 350° F. Lightly coat an 8x8-inch baking pan with nonstick vegetable-oil spray. In a large bowl, combine the whole-wheat flour, all-purpose flour, sugar, cocoa powder, and baking powder. In a medium bowl, beat the egg whites until foamy; add the baby-food prunes, buttermilk, and vanilla. Add the egg mixture to the flour mixture and mix until blended. Stir in the chocolate chips. Spread batter in the prepared baking pan and sprinkle the walnuts on top. Bake 25 minutes, or until a toothpick inserted near the center comes out clean. Let cool, in the pan, on a wire rack.

Lemon Bars

Macaroon Brownies, Cheesecake Brownies, and Black Forest Brownies

Crispy Nutty Bars

Easy Truffles

Chewy Fruity Molasses Bars

Makes 24 bars

ⰔⰔ Ⱄ Ⱄ Ⱄ

My two-year-old nephew loves these bars. The whole-wheat flour and dried fruit make them a wholesome treat. Psst, these have prunes, too. I don't know why people often wrinkle their noses when prunes are mentioned, but because they do, I don't usually broadcast this ingredient. In fact, someone once said of these bars that the "big raisins" were great!

How fat and calories were lowered:

ⱱ Used fat-free cream cheese instead of butter

ⱱ Used less walnuts

ⱱ Replaced the whole egg with an egg white

Nutrition Scorecard *(per bar)*	Before	After
Calories	187	147
Fat (grams)	7	3
% calories from fat	33	14
Cholesterol (mg)	19	0

1 cup whole-wheat flour

½ cup all-purpose flour

¼ cup quick oats

½ teaspoon baking soda

½ teaspoon ground nutmeg

1 cup snipped pitted prunes (½-inch pieces)

¾ cup chopped walnuts

½ cup chopped dried apricots

½ cup raisins

4 ounces fat-free cream cheese, softened at room temperature

1 cup packed dark brown sugar

1 egg white

½ cup mild molasses

Preheat the oven to 350° F. Lightly coat a 13x9-inch baking pan with nonstick vegetable-oil spray. In a small bowl, combine the whole-wheat flour, all-purpose flour, oats, baking soda, and nutmeg; set aside. In a large bowl, combine the prunes, walnuts, apricots, and raisins. Add about 2 tablespoons of the flour mixture and stir to coat the dried fruits and nuts. Set aside.

In a large bowl, cream the fat-free cream cheese and brown sugar with an electric mixer until light. Beat in the egg white until blended. Gradually beat in the molasses and the flour mixture on low speed, just until blended. Using a rubber spatula, fold in the floured dried fruits and nuts until blended. Spread the batter in the prepared pan. Bake for 30 minutes, or until the edges begin to pull away from the sides of the pan. Let cool, in the pan, on a wire rack before cutting into bars.

Cheesecake Brownies

Makes 12 brownies

✄✄✄✄✄

*S*uch *a pretty brownie and so easy to make. It's hard to believe it has only 2 grams of fat.*

How fat and calories were lowered:

☞ Replaced the butter with a combination of applesauce and buttermilk

☞ Used egg whites in place of whole eggs

☞ Used a combination of light cream cheese and nonfat cottage cheese instead of regular cream cheese

Nutrition Scorecard *(per brownie)*		
	Before	*After*
Calories	262	152
Fat (grams)	15	2
% calories from fat	51	11
Cholesterol (mg)	77	4

Cheesecake Mixture

½ cup nonfat cottage cheese

4 ounces tub-style light cream cheese

⅓ cup sugar

2 teaspoons all-purpose flour

2 egg whites

¼ teaspoon vanilla extract

Brownie

½ cup whole-wheat flour

¼ cup all-purpose flour

½ cup unsweetened cocoa powder

1 cup sugar

½ teaspoon baking powder

⅓ cup buttermilk

⅓ cup unsweetened applesauce

4 egg whites

1 teaspoon vanilla extract

Preheat the oven to 325° F. Lightly coat an 8x8-inch baking pan with nonstick vegetable-oil spray.

To make the cheesecake mixture: In a food processor or blender, puree the cottage cheese until smooth. Add the light cream cheese, sugar, flour, egg whites, and vanilla and pulse until blended. Set aside.

To make the brownie mixture: In a large bowl, combine the whole-wheat flour, all-purpose flour, cocoa, sugar, and baking powder; set aside. In a small bowl, combine the buttermilk, applesauce, egg whites, and vanilla; mix thoroughly. Add liquid mixture to flour mixture and stir until well blended.

To assemble: Transfer the brownie batter to the prepared pan. Top with the cheesecake mixture. Using a knife, create a marbleized effect by carving S shapes vertically and horizontally. Bake for 35 to 40 minutes, or until lightly golden.

A Screaming Sweet Tooth—Why It Happens

It's not unusual for people to get a sweet tooth when they have undereaten in some way. They may not have consumed enough calories, they may have had too few carbohydrates, or perhaps they just went too long between meals. Some researchers speculate that the sweet tooth is actually nature's insurance to get us to eat—the body is trying to seduce its owner into excessive indulgence, of sweet, calorically dense foods. To make the most of a sweet tooth, consider the following:

- Start eating breakfast, even if you're not hungry. Researcher John Foreyt, Ph.D., an expert in obesity, has found that if people eat breakfast seven days in a row, by the eighth day they usually feel hunger in the morning.

- When you do decide to eat something sweet, sit and savor the experience. Enjoy the food moment rather than feeling guilty. Remember, one food, one meal, or one day will not make or break your health.

- Eat your treat with or after a meal. If you eat a treat when you're ravenous, you're more apt to overeat, not because of lack of willpower but rather because of sheer hunger.

- Never go longer than five hours without eating—that's when you're most apt to enter the zone of primal hunger, and once you're at that point, healthy thoughts usually fly out the window.

- Make sure you are getting enough carbohydrates, which at times have had the undeserved bad reputation for being fattening. Minimally, you need six grain servings each day. One serving is, for instance, one slice of bread, one tortilla, or one-half cup of pasta, cereal, or rice.

- If your sweet tooth is chronic and unrelenting, you may want to look a little deeper. Sometimes a sweet tooth is really about other issues—a reward for a tough day, a time-out from a boring job.

Crispy Nutty Bars

Makes 32 bars

⋈ ⋈ ⋈ ⋈ ⋈

This easy three-layer dessert is especially popular with kids. Mini marshmallows are sandwiched between a peanut bar and crisp rice topping.

How fat and calories were lowered:

☞ Replaced the butter with a combination of peanut butter and fat-free cream cheese in the dough

☞ Used an egg white instead of egg yolks

☞ Reduced the amount of peanut butter chips

☞ Reduced the amount of peanuts and then chopped them for even distribution

☞ Eliminated the butter in the topping

Nutrition Scorecard *(per bar)*		
	Before	*After*
Calories	242	162
Fat (grams)	13	5
% calories from fat	47	29
Cholesterol (mg)	25	0

Bars

1 cup all-purpose flour

½ cup whole-wheat flour

¼ teaspoon baking powder

¼ teaspoon baking soda

¼ cup crunchy peanut butter
    (natural-style)

2 ounces fat-free cream cheese (brick-style)

1 egg white

1 teaspoon vanilla extract

⅔ cup packed light brown sugar

3 cups miniature marshmallows

Topping

¾ cup dry roasted peanuts

1¼ cups peanut butter chips

⅔ cup light corn syrup

2 teaspoons vanilla extract

2 cups crisp rice cereal (such as
    Rice Krispies)

Preheat the oven to 350° F. Lightly coat a 13x9x2-inch baking pan with nonstick vegetable-oil spray; set aside.

To make the bars: In a small bowl, combine the all-purpose flour, whole-wheat flour, baking powder, and baking soda; set aside. In a large bowl, cream together the peanut butter and fat-free cream cheese. Add the egg white and vanilla and beat well. Mix in the brown sugar and beat until fluffy. Add the flour mixture and beat on low speed until crumbly. With wet fingertips, firmly press the mixture into the prepared pan. Bake 12 to 15 minutes, or until golden brown. Remove from oven. Immediately sprinkle the marshmallows over the surface. Return to the oven for 1 to 2 minutes more, or just until the marshmallows begin to puff. Remove from the oven and let cool, in the pan, on a wire rack while you prepare the topping.

To make the topping: Coarsely chop the peanuts; set aside. In a large microwavable bowl, melt the peanut butter chips, stirring every 30 seconds. Add the corn syrup and mix well until smooth. Stir in the crisp rice cereal and chopped nuts. Immediately spread the cereal mixture by tablespoonfuls over the marshmallow layer. Cover and refrigerate about 2 hours, or until firm. Cut into bars. Store in a covered container.

Brown sugar is made by simply mixing white sugar crystals with molasses.

❧ ❧ ❧ ❧ ❧

Pecan Bars

Makes 16 bars

⋈ ⋈ ⋈ ⋈

Great pecan flavor with half the calories.
How fat and calories were lowered:

☞ Replaced the butter with a combination of buttermilk, chopped pecans, and oil

☞ Reduced the amount of sugar

☞ Reduced the amount of pecans

Nutrition Scorecard *(per bar)*		
	Before	After
Calories	303	148
Fat (grams)	18	6
% calories from fat	50	33
Cholesterol (mg)	52	0

Bars

1 cup whole-wheat flour

½ cup powdered sugar

3 tablespoons finely chopped pecans

⅛ teaspoon cinnamon

⅓ cup buttermilk

1 tablespoon canola oil

Pecan Topping

¼ cup packed light brown sugar

¼ cup white sugar

⅓ cup light corn syrup

2 egg whites

1 teaspoon vanilla extract

⅛ teaspoon salt

¾ cup chopped pecans

Preheat the oven to 350° F. Lightly coat a 9-inch square baking pan with nonstick vegetable-oil spray.

To make the bars: In a medium bowl, combine the flour, powdered sugar, pecans, and cinnamon. In a measuring cup, mix together the buttermilk and oil. Add the buttermilk mixture to the flour mixture and, using an electric mixer, beat until thoroughly combined. Using wet fingertips or the back of a large spoon, press the dough into the bottom of the prepared pan and ½ inch up the sides. Bake 10 to 12 minutes, or until lightly golden. Remove from the oven and let cool, in the pan, on a wire rack.

To make the pecan topping: In a small bowl, whisk together both sugars and the corn syrup, egg whites, vanilla, and salt until blended. Stir in the pecans. Pour the topping evenly over the bars. Bake the bars until the topping is set and forms a crust, about 25 minutes. Allow the bars to cool for 15 minutes, in the pan, on a wire rack, then run a knife around the sides of the pan. Let the bars cool completely and cut into squares.

Lemon Bars

Makes 20 bars

⊱⊰⊱⊰⊱

I love lemon bars and am always tinkering around with them. This is one of my favorite versions.

How the fat and calories were lowered:

☞ Replaced the butter in the crust with a combination of buttermilk and oil

☞ Used egg substitute in place of whole eggs (the egg substitute also serves to add a nice lemony color)

Nutrition Scorecard
(per bar)

	Before	After
Calories	108	86
Fat (grams)	5	2
% calories from fat	52	19
Cholesterol (mg)	34	trace

Bars

½ cup whole-wheat flour

½ cup all-purpose flour

¼ cup sugar

1 teaspoon finely grated lemon zest

¼ cup finely chopped walnuts

⅓ cup buttermilk

1 tablespoon canola oil

Lemon Topping

½ cup fat-free egg substitute, frozen, thawed

2 tablespoons all-purpose flour

¾ cup sugar

2½ teaspoons finely grated lemon zest

3 tablespoons fresh lemon juice

¼ teaspoon baking powder

Powdered sugar, for sifting over top

Preheat the oven to 350° F. Lightly coat an 8x8x2-inch baking pan with nonstick vegetable-oil spray.

To make the bars: In a medium bowl, combine the whole-wheat flour, the ½ cup all-purpose flour, the ¼ cup sugar, the 1 teaspoon lemon zest, and the walnuts. In a small bowl, whisk together the buttermilk and oil; drizzle into flour mixture. Using a pastry blender or fork, cut in buttermilk mixture. Press the dough into the bottom of the pan. Bake for 12 to 15 minutes, or until light brown on the edges.

To make the lemon topping: In a small bowl, combine the thawed egg substitute, the 2 tablespoons all-purpose flour, the ¾ cup sugar, the 2½ teaspoons lemon zest, the juice, and the baking powder. Using an electric mixer on medium speed, beat for 2 minutes, or until thoroughly combined. Pour the topping over the hot baked layer. Bake in 350° F. oven 20 minutes more, or until the bars are light brown around the edges and the center is set. Let cool, in the pan, on a wire rack. Sift powdered sugar over top. Cut into bars.

Incredible

❧ ❧ ❧ ❧ ❧

Cookies

Crispy Orange Lace Cookies

Makes 30 cookies

❧❧❧❧❧

At last, a crispy low-fat cookie that only takes 4 minutes to bake! And they are absolutely irresistible. Take care not to make the cookies too big, or you will have difficulty removing them from the cookie sheet.

How fat and calories were lowered:

- Greatly reduced the amount of butter and used the light version

- Replaced the whole eggs with egg whites

Nutrition Scorecard *(per cookie)*	Before	After
Calories	68	40
Fat (grams)	4	1
% calories from fat	53	22
Cholesterol (mg)	6	1

1 cup quick oats	⅓ cup sugar
⅓ cup light corn syrup	1 teaspoon vanilla extract
1 tablespoon canola oil	2 tablespoons all-purpose flour
2 tablespoons light butter	1 teaspoon baking powder
2 egg whites	1 teaspoon finely grated orange zest

Preheat the oven to 400° F. Lightly coat two baking sheets with nonstick vegetable-oil spray and dust with flour; shake off excess.

In a medium bowl, combine the oats, corn syrup, and oil. In a small saucepan, melt the light butter over medium heat. Cook until it begins to turn a light, nutty brown, being careful not to burn it. Pour the butter into the oat mixture and stir to combine. Set aside.

In a medium bowl, beat together the egg whites and sugar with an electric mixer until opaque and thickened, about 3 minutes. Blend in the vanilla.

In a large bowl, stir together the flour, baking powder, and orange zest; fold in the egg white mixture. Add the oat mixture and stir gently to combine.

Using a 1-teaspoon measuring spoon, transfer the batter by heaping teaspoonfuls onto the prepared baking sheets, placing the cookies about 2 inches apart. Bake, one sheet at a time, for about 4 minutes, or until golden.

Let cool on the baking sheet for 2 minutes, then carefully remove cookies with a spatula and let cool on a flat surface (not a rack).

Chocolate Chip Almond Coconut Cookies

Makes 48 cookies

✄ ✄ ✄ ✄ ✄

Another recipe no one can believe is low in fat!
How fat and calories were lowered:

☛ Used light butter and less of it

☛ Reduced the amount of almonds

☛ Replaced whole eggs with egg whites

☛ Used fewer chocolate chips and switched to the mini size

Nutrition Scorecard *(per cookie)*	Before	After
Calories	116	93
Fat (grams)	7	3
% calories from fat	52	29
Cholesterol (mg)	7	4

1 cup all-purpose flour

1 cup whole-wheat flour

½ cup quick oats

1 teaspoon baking soda

2 tablespoons light butter, at room
    temperature

¾ cup packed light brown sugar

1 teaspoon vanilla extract

4 egg whites, slightly beaten

½ cup sugar

⅓ cup light corn syrup

¾ cup flaked coconut, toasted

⅔ cup chopped almonds, toasted

1 cup mini chocolate chips

Preheat the oven to 375° F. Spray two baking sheets with nonstick vegetable-oil spray.

In a medium bowl, combine the all-purpose flour, whole-wheat flour, oats, and baking soda; set aside.

In a large bowl, cream together the light butter, brown sugar, and vanilla until pastelike; set aside.

In another large bowl, beat the egg whites with the sugar until thick and opaque. Stir in the corn syrup. Combine the egg white mixture with the brown sugar mixture; mix well. Gradually stir in the flour mixture. Stir in the coconut, almonds, and chocolate chips.

Drop the cookie dough by heaping teaspoonfuls onto the prepared cookie sheets, at least 1 inch apart (cookies will spread). Bake 7 to 8 minutes, until golden. Remove from the oven. Let cool 5 minutes before removing from baking sheets. Transfer to wax paper.

Oatmeal Pecan Cookies

Makes 48 cookies

❧❧❧❧❧

The sweet, aromatic pecans accent these maple-scented cookies.
How fat and calories were lowered:

☞ Eliminated the butter and replaced it in part with corn syrup

☞ Reduced the amount of nuts and toasted the nuts to enhance the flavor

☞ Replaced whole eggs with egg whites

☞ Reduced the amount of sugar

Nutrition Scorecard (per cookie)		
	Before	*After*
Calories	84	64
Fat (grams)	5	2
% calories from fat	49	20
Cholesterol (mg)	8	0

3 cups quick oats	⅓ cup light corn syrup
1 cup all-purpose flour	¼ cup mild molasses
1 teaspoon cinnamon	3 egg whites, lightly beaten
½ teaspoon baking soda	1 teaspoon maple extract
¾ cup packed light brown sugar	⅔ cup toasted pecans

Preheat the oven to 350° F. Lightly coat two baking sheets with nonstick vegetable-oil spray.

In a large bowl, combine the oats, flour, cinnamon, and baking soda; set aside.

In a medium bowl, blend together the brown sugar, corn syrup, molasses, egg whites, and maple extract with an electric mixer at medium speed. Combine the egg white mixture with the oat mixture. Stir in the pecans. Bake for 8 to 10 minutes, until light brown.

Quick Tip

Since recipes taste so much better with **toasted** nuts, save yourself some time by toasting a whole batch, and freeze what you don't use.

❧❧❧❧❧

Butterscotch Chip Cookies

Makes 48 cookies

✄✄ ✄✄ ✄✄

The maple extract helps bring out the rich flavor of butterscotch chips. How fat and calories were reduced:

☞ Used less butterscotch chips

☞ Replaced butter with a combination of corn syrup and molasses

Nutrition Scorecard
(per cookie)

	Before	After
Calories	101	64
Fat (grams)	5	2
% calories from fat	44	20
Cholesterol (mg)	8	0

3 cups quick oats

1 cup all-purpose flour

1 teaspoon cinnamon

½ teaspoon baking soda

¾ cup packed light brown sugar

⅓ cup light corn syrup

¼ cup mild molasses

3 egg whites, lightly beaten

1 teaspoon maple extract

1½ cup butterscotch chips

Preheat the oven to 350° F. Lightly coat two baking sheets with nonstick vegetable-oil spray.

In a large bowl, combine the oats, flour, cinnamon, and baking soda; set aside.

In a medium bowl, blend together the brown sugar, corn syrup, molasses, egg whites, and maple extract with an electric mixer at medium speed. Combine egg mixture with oat mixture. Stir in the butterscotch chips. Drop by rounded teaspoonfuls onto the prepared baking sheets. Bake for 8 to 10 minutes, until light brown.

Crispy Almond Lace Cookies

Makes 40 cookies

✄ ✄ ✄ ✄

Toasting the almonds makes this delicate cookie absolutely irresistible.
How the fat and calories were lowered:

☞ Eliminated butter and replaced it in part with canola oil

☞ Reduced the amount of almonds and toasted them

Nutrition Scorecard
(per cookie)

	Before	After
Calories	91	40
Fat (grams)	6	1
% calories from fat	53	29
Cholesterol (mg)	8	0

1 cup quick oats

⅓ cup plus 2 tablespoons light corn syrup

1 tablespoon oil, preferably canola oil

2 egg whites

⅓ cup sugar

½ teaspoon almond extract

2 tablespoons all-purpose flour

1 teaspoon baking powder

½ cup chopped almonds, toasted

Preheat the oven to 400° F. Lightly coat three baking sheets with nonstick vegetable-oil spray and dust with flour; shake off excess.

In a medium bowl, combine the oats, corn syrup, and oil. Set aside.

In another medium bowl, beat together the egg whites and sugar with an electric mixer until opaque and thickened, about 3 minutes. Blend in the almond extract.

In a small bowl, stir together the flour and baking powder; stir into the egg mixture. Add the rolled oat mixture; stir gently to combine. Mix in the toasted almonds.

Use a 1-teaspoon measuring spoon to transfer the batter, about 2 inches apart, onto the prepared baking sheets. Bake, one sheet at a time, for about 4 minutes, or until the cookies are golden. Let cool on the baking sheet for 2 minutes, then carefully remove cookies and let cool on a flat surface (not a rack).

Jam Thumbprint Cookies

Makes 36 cookies

✥ ✥ ✥ ✥ ✥

I enjoy making these cookies with my daughter for the holidays. Kids love to do the thumbprint part.

How fat and calories were lowered:

☛ Used a combination of light butter and fat-free cream cheese instead of butter

☛ Incorporated whole-wheat flour for nutrition boost

Nutrition Scorecard		
(per cookie)		
	Before	*After*
Calories	102	67
Fat *(grams)*	7	2
% calories from fat	61	30
Cholesterol *(mg)*	14	4

---

1 cup whole-wheat flour	4 ounces fat-free cream cheese
1 cup all-purpose flour	½ cup sugar
½ cup finely chopped walnuts	1 teaspoon vanilla extract
½ cup light butter, at room temperature	⅓ cup jam or preserves

Preheat the oven to 350° F. Lightly coat two baking sheets with nonstick vegetable-oil spray.

Combine the whole-wheat flour, all-purpose flour, and walnuts; set aside.

In a large bowl, cream together the light butter, fat-free cream cheese, and sugar. Add the vanilla and stir in the flour mixture. Shape the dough into 1-inch balls. Press centers with thumb; fill depression with about ½ teaspoon jam; and set cookies on baking sheets, about 2 inches apart.

Bake for 10 to 12 minutes, or until light golden brown. Let cool on wire rack.

Chocolate Meringue Cookies

Makes 48 cookies

This cookie can satisfy my chocolate craving like no other. It has a puffy, featherweight appearance on the outside, but it's packed with chocolate flavor on the inside.

How fat and calories were lowered:

- Used mini chocolate chips and less of them
- Reduced the amount of nuts

Nutrition Scorecard
(per cookie)

	Before	After
Calories	44	35
Fat (grams)	2	1
% calories from fat	40	30
Cholesterol (mg)	0	0

3 egg whites	3 tablespoons unsweetened cocoa powder
⅛ teaspoon cream of tartar	½ cup mini semisweet chocolate chips
1 cup sugar	⅓ cup finely chopped hazelnuts or walnuts

Preheat the oven to 250° F. Lightly coat two baking sheets with nonstick vegetable-oil spray and lightly dust with flour.

In a large bowl, beat the egg whites with an electric mixer until foamy, add the cream of tartar, and beat until soft peaks form. Gradually sprinkle in the sugar, 1 tablespoon at a time, beating well after each addition. Sift the cocoa over the meringue batter. With a rubber spatula, fold in the cocoa powder, chocolate chips, and nuts. Drop by the teaspoonful onto the prepared cookie sheets.

Bake for 25 to 30 minutes, or until crisp. Let the cookies cool on the baking sheets for 2 minutes, then transfer carefully to wire racks to cool completely.

Peanut Butter Cookies

Makes 36 cookies

⋈ ⋈ ⋈ ⋈ ⋈

These cookies are a sure bet for satisfying a yen for peanut butter, especially with the hidden peanut butter chips. (Tip: You can chill the dough for 30 minutes to make it easier to handle.)

How fat and calories were lowered:

☛ Eliminated the butter and replaced it in part with corn syrup (granulated sugar was reduced)

☛ Reduced the amount of peanut butter chips and nuts

☛ Used egg whites instead of a whole egg

☛ Used a reduced-fat peanut butter

Nutrition Scorecard
(per cookie)

	Before	After
Calories	136	100
Fat (grams)	7	3
% calories from fat	48	29
Cholesterol (mg)	13	0

1 cup all-purpose flour

¾ cup whole-wheat flour

½ teaspoon baking powder

½ teaspoon baking soda

⅛ teaspoon salt

½ cup reduced-fat smooth peanut butter (natural-style)

⅓ cup light corn syrup

½ cup packed light brown sugar

⅓ cup sugar

2 egg whites

2 tablespoons fresh orange juice

1 teaspoon vanilla extract

⅔ cup peanut butter chips

⅓ cup chopped peanuts

Preheat the oven to 375° F. Lightly coat two baking sheets with nonstick vegetable-oil spray.

In a medium bowl, combine the all-purpose flour, whole-wheat flour, baking powder, baking soda, and salt; set aside.

In a large mixing bowl, beat together the peanut butter, corn syrup, brown sugar, and white sugar. Beat in the egg whites. Add the orange juice and vanilla. Gradually beat in the flour mixture, blending thoroughly. Stir in the peanut butter chips.

Shape the dough into 1-inch balls. (This works best if you lightly wet your hands.) Arrange dough balls 2 inches apart on the prepared baking sheets. Flatten the balls with a wet fork. Sprinkle with the chopped peanuts.

Bake for 10 to 12 minutes, or until golden. Let the cookies cool for 2 minutes on the baking sheets, then transfer them carefully to a wire rack to cool completely.

Molasses Chews

Makes 36 cookies

⋈ ⋈ ⋈ ⋈ ⋈

Delightfully chewy and spicy cookies. It was after tasting one of these wholesome treats that my fifteen-month-old learned to say "cookie." How fat and calories were lowered:

☛ Used light butter in place of butter

☛ Eliminated egg

Nutrition Scorecard *(per cookie)*		
	Before	*After*
Calories	98	75
Fat (grams)	4	2
% calories from fat	37	23
Cholesterol (mg)	16	5

1 ¼ cups all-purpose flour

1 cup whole-wheat flour

1 teaspoon cinnamon

½ teaspoon ground ginger

¼ teaspoon ground cloves

¼ teaspoon ground allspice

¾ cup light butter

½ cup packed dark brown sugar

½ cup sugar, plus 2 tablespoons for
      sprinkling on cookies before baking

⅓ cup mild molasses

Preheat the oven to 400° F. Lightly coat two baking sheets with vegetable-oil spray.

In a medium bowl, combine the all-purpose flour, whole-wheat flour, cinnamon, ginger, cloves, and allspice; set aside.

In a large mixing bowl, beat together the light butter, the brown sugar, and the ½ cup white sugar until creamy. Add the molasses. Stir in the flour mixture, blending thoroughly. Cover the dough and chill it for 30 minutes.

Scoop out rounded teaspoonfuls of dough and shape them into balls, then flatten into 2-inch disks and place on the prepared baking sheets. Sprinkle with the 2 tablespoons sugar.

Bake for 8 to 10 minutes, or until lightly browned. Let the cookies cool for 2 minutes on the baking sheets. Transfer them carefully to a wire rack to cool completely.

Three-Layer Fudge Bars

Makes 80 bars

✄ ✄ ✄ ✄ ✄

Every Christmas, my brothers-in law would beg me to make the original version of this recipe. Naturally, I had to get their thumbs-up before I published this made-over creation. To my surprise (and theirs), they like this version even better.

How fat and calories were lowered:

☛ Eliminated butter

☛ Used light peanut butter and less of it

☛ Replaced nuts with crisp rice cereal

☛ Used evaporated skim milk instead of whole milk

Nutrition Scorecard *(per bar)*		
	Before	After
Calories	175	106
Fat (grams)	10	4
% calories from fat	53	33
Cholesterol (mg)	7	0

1 (12-ounce) package (2 cups) semisweet chocolate chips

1 (12-ounce) package (2 cups) butterscotch chips

1 cup reduced-fat peanut butter (natural-style)

2 cups crisp rice cereal (such as Rice Krispies)

½ cup evaporated skim milk

1 (4.6 ounce) package cook-and-serve vanilla pudding mix (not instant)

1½ pounds powdered sugar

1 teaspoon vanilla extract

Line a 15x10-inch jelly roll pan with foil. (Do *not* apply nonstick vegetable-oil spray—it causes the chocolate to adhere.) In a large microwavable bowl, melt the chocolate and butterscotch chips in the microwave on High setting, stirring thoroughly every 30 seconds. Stir in the peanut butter and mix well. Spread half of the mixture in the prepared pan; chill. Stir cereal into remaining chocolate mixture; set aside.

In a large saucepan, heat the evaporated milk over medium heat and stir in the pudding mix. Cook, stirring constantly, until mixture is slightly thickened. (*Do not boil.*) Remove from the heat. Gradually stir in the powdered sugar and vanilla; let cool slightly. Carefully transfer the pudding mixture (it will be very thick) by tablespoonfuls over the chilled chocolate layer until evenly distributed. Lightly press the pudding layer with the back of wooden spoon into the chocolate. Chill 15 minutes.

Drop reserved chocolate-cereal mixture by tablespoonfuls over chilled pudding layer; spread to cover. Chill until firm; cut into bars. Store tightly wrapped in refrigerator.

Easy Truffles

Makes 48 truffles

✖ ✖ ✖ ✖ ✖

This is an incredibly easy recipe. It requires no oven or stovetop, so it's a favorite of mine to make around the holidays. I'm not usually a fan of fat-free cream cheese, but it works very well in these truffles by providing a smooth texture. I added a bit of instant coffee to intensify the chocolate flavor.

How fat and calories were lowered:

☛ Substituted fat-free cream cheese in place of the regular version

☛ Replaced nut coating with sweetened cocoa

Nutrition Scorecard (per truffle)		
	Before	*After*
Calories	100	70
Fat (grams)	6	3
% calories from fat	54	34
Cholesterol (mg)	5	0

1 (12-ounce) package semisweet chocolate chips

8 ounces fat-free cream cheese, softened

3 cups powdered sugar

1 teaspoon instant coffee granules

1 teaspoon nonfat milk

1 teaspoon vanilla extract

½ cup sweet ground chocolate or unsweetened cocoa powder

In a large microwavable bowl, melt the chocolate chips in the microwave, on High setting, stirring thoroughly every 30 seconds; set aside.

With an electric mixer on Medium setting, beat the fat-free cream cheese until smooth. Gradually add the sugar, beating until well blended. Dissolve the instant coffee in the nonfat milk; stir it into the cream cheese mixture. Add the vanilla and melted chocolate. Refrigerate about 15 minutes. Shape into 1-inch balls. Sift the sweet ground chocolate over truffle balls. Store in refrigerator.

Cinnayum Cookies

Makes 48 cookies

✂ ✂ ✂ ✂ ✂

These cinnamony cookies are a family favorite. I found that using light butter preserved the buttery flavor with half the fat. But you cannot simply substitute light butter in baking without adjusting for its extra liquid (don't worry—that's already been done here for you). Whole-wheat flour is used to add a nutritional kick.

How fat and calories were lowered:

✍ Replaced butter with a combination of light butter and corn syrup

✍ Used an egg white instead of a whole egg

Nutrition Scorecard
(per cookie)

	Before	After
Calories	88	62
Fat (grams)	4	1
% calories from fat	42	21
Cholesterol (mg)	19	4

Cookies

1¾ cups all-purpose flour

1 cup whole-wheat flour

¼ teaspoon salt

¼ teaspoon cinnamon

¾ cup light butter

1 cup sugar

¼ cup light corn syrup

1 egg white

1 teaspoon vanilla extract

Topping

1 tablespoon cinnamon

3 tablespoons sugar

Preheat the oven to 375° F. Lightly coat four baking sheets with nonstick vegetable-oil spray.

In a medium bowl, combine the all-purpose flour, whole-wheat flour, salt, and ¼ teaspoon cinnamon; set aside.

In a large bowl, beat together the light butter and 1 cup sugar until creamy. Add the corn syrup and beat well. Add the egg white and vanilla. Stir in the flour mixture, blending thoroughly.

Shape the dough into 1-inch balls. Combine the 1 tablespoon cinnamon and 3 tablespoons sugar. Roll the dough balls in the mixture. Flatten the dough balls into disks and place on the prepared baking sheets. Bake for 10 to 12 minutes, or until golden. Let cool on the baking sheets for 2 minutes. Remove the cookies to wire racks to cool completely.

Rocky Road Fudge Surprise

Makes 60 pieces

❧❧❧❧❧

The surprise in this delicious fudge is baby-food prunes. This chocolaty-looking substitution helps to maintain a smooth texture without all the fat. I love to see people taste this goody and . . . rave and then watch their eyes roll back when I tell them how this fudge got healthier! (By the way, never divulge the surprise to guests until after their taste buds are in heaven.) I prefer using the large marshmallows and cutting them into quarters rather than using the miniatures—the texture of the miniatures is not quite the same.

How fat and calories were reduced:

Nutrition Scorecard (per piece)		
	Before	After
Calories	125	96
Fat (grams)	6	3
% calories from fat	41	30
Cholesterol (mg)	7	1

☛ Used evaporated skim milk instead of whole canned milk

☛ Replaced most of the butter with baby-food prunes

☛ Reduced the amount of sugar by ½ cup

☛ Reduced the amount of nuts

2 tablespoons butter

⅔ cup evaporated skim milk

2½ cups sugar

1 (12-ounce) package semisweet chocolate chips

1 (2½-ounce) jar baby-food prunes

1 (7½-ounce) jar marshmallow creme

1 teaspoon vanilla extract

¾ cup chopped walnuts, divided use

20 marshmallows (2 cups), cut into quarters

Line a 13x9-inch pan with wax paper and set aside.

In a large saucepan, melt the butter. Stir in the milk and sugar and bring to a boil over medium heat, stirring constantly. Boil for 5 minutes, stirring constantly and carefully. Remove the pan from the heat and gradually stir in the chocolate chips. Add baby-food prunes, marshmallow creme, vanilla, and ½ cup of the walnuts. Gently stir in the quartered marshmallows. Pour the chocolate mixture into the prepared pan, top with the remaining nuts, and chill.

Wendy's Cookies

Makes 36 cookies

❄❄❄❄❄

I'll never forget Wendy's party. The next day all I heard about was her cookies—even from friends who don't generally rave about food. So of course not only did I insist that Wendy make me some of her famous cookies, I also got ahold of her recipe. I've played with this recipe many times to finally get the lower-fat, lower-calorie version right—it's one of my favorites.

How fat and calories were lowered:

🖝 Replaced butter with a combination of light butter and fat-free cream cheese

🖝 Used egg whites instead of whole eggs

🖝 Reduced amount of chocolate chips by more than half, and mini chips were used to better distribute the chocolate

🖝 Reduced the amount of coconut and butterscotch chips

Nutrition Scorecard
(per cookie)

	Before	After
Calories	169	103
Fat (grams)	10	4
% calories from fat	51	31
Cholesterol (mg)	22	5

1 cup all-purpose flour

¼ teaspoon salt

¼ teaspoon ground nutmeg

4 ounces fat-free cream cheese

¼ cup light butter

½ cup white sugar

⅓ cup packed light brown sugar

2 egg whites

1 teaspoon vanilla extract

2 cups quick oats

⅔ cup mini chocolate chips

¾ cup butterscotch chips

¾ cup flaked coconut

Preheat the oven to 375° F. Lightly coat three baking sheets with nonstick vegetable-oil spray.

In a small bowl, combine the flour, salt, and nutmeg; set aside.

In a large bowl, using an electric mixer, beat together the cream cheese, light butter, white sugar, and brown sugar. Add the egg whites and vanilla. Blend well. Mix in the flour mixture. Stir in the oats until well blended, then stir in the chocolate chips, butterscotch chips, and coconut.

Drop the cookie dough by the tablespoonful onto the prepared baking sheets. Gently flatten with the back side of a fork. Bake 10 to 12 minutes, or until golden.

Chocolate Turtle Pecan Cookies

Makes 24 cookies

✄✄✄✄✄

*These fancy caramel-topped cookies are absolutely delicious.
How fat and calories were lowered:*

✒ Replaced butter with a combination of light butter and
fat-free cream cheese

✒ Reduced amount of pecans

✒ Eliminated chocolate chips

✒ Used fewer caramels

✒ Replaced heavy cream with evaporated skim milk

Nutrition Scorecard		
(per cookie)		
	Before	After
Calories	160	86
Fat *(grams)*	10	4
% calories from fat	55	36
Cholesterol *(mg)*	22	3

Cookies

1 cup all-purpose flour

⅓ cup unsweetened cocoa powder

⅛ teaspoon salt

⅔ cup sugar

¼ cup light butter

2 ounces fat-free cream cheese

1 egg white

2 tablespoons nonfat milk

1 teaspoon vanilla extract

1 egg white, slightly beaten

¾ cup finely chopped pecans, toasted

Caramel Topping

5 caramels, unwrapped

5 teaspoons evaporated skim milk

To make the cookies: In a small bowl, combine the flour, cocoa, and salt; set aside.

In a large bowl, beat together the sugar, light butter, fat-free cream cheese, 1 egg white, nonfat milk, and vanilla. Add the flour mixture and blend well. Chill dough at least 30 minutes, or until firm enough to handle.

Preheat the oven to 350° F. Lightly coat two baking sheets with nonstick vegetable-oil spray. Shape the dough into 1-inch balls. Dip each ball into the remaining egg white and roll in pecans to coat. Place on prepared baking sheet and gently flatten.

Bake 10 to 12 minutes. Let cookies cool on baking sheets for 2 minutes and then carefully remove to wire racks to cool completely.

To make the caramel topping: In a small saucepan, combine caramels and evaporated skim milk. Cook over low heat, stirring frequently, until caramels are melted and mixture is smooth. Drizzle caramel topping over cooled cookies.

Oatmeal Raisin Cookies

Makes 48 cookies

✄✄✄✄✄

These old-fashioned cookies make a cozy treat, especially when paired up with a cool glass of nonfat milk. Whole-wheat flour is added for more whole-grain goodness.

How fat and calories were lowered:

- Replaced solid shortening with a combination of fat-free cream cheese, molasses, and oil

- Reduced amount of nuts and toasted them for extra flavor

- Reduced amount of sugar

Nutrition Scorecard *(per cookie)*		
	Before	After
Calories	137	94
Fat (grams)	6	2
% calories from fat	40	21
Cholesterol (mg)	9	0

---

1 cup all-purpose flour

½ cup whole-wheat flour

1 teaspoon cinnamon

¼ teaspoon ground nutmeg

¼ teaspoon baking soda

4 ounces fat-free cream cheese, at room temperature

¼ cup mild molasses

3 tablespoons canola oil

1 cup packed light brown sugar

⅓ cup white sugar

3 egg whites

1 teaspoon vanilla extract

3 cups quick oats

1¼ cups seedless raisins

⅔ cup chopped walnuts, toasted

Preheat the oven to 350° F. Lightly coat four baking sheets with nonstick vegetable-oil spray.

In a small bowl, combine all-purpose flour, whole-wheat flour, cinnamon, nutmeg, and baking soda; set aside.

In a large bowl, cream together the fat-free cream cheese, molasses, oil, and white and brown sugars. Stir in egg whites and vanilla. Add flour mixture to sugar mixture. Stir in the oats, then the raisins and walnuts.

Drop the cookie dough by rounded teaspoonfuls onto the prepared baking sheets. Flatten with the back of a wet fork or spoon.

Bake for 10 to 12 minutes, or until golden. Transfer to wire rack to cool.

Chilly

Desserts—

Frozen and

Refreshing

Peanut Butter Ice Cream Squares

Serves 16

✄ ✄ ✄ ✄ ✄

A creamy peanut butter ribbon runs through the middle of this easy-to-make treat. Be sure to toast the nuts for the crust and filling at the same time. Tip: To melt jam, place in a microwave for 10 to 15 seconds.

How fat and calories were lowered:

☛ Replaced butter with melted jam

☛ Used nugget cereal for part of the crust

☛ Replaced ice cream with fat-free ice cream or frozen yogurt

☛ Reduced the amount of nuts and toasted them to enhance peanutty flavor

Nutrition Scorecard
(per square)

	Before	After
Calories	290	186
Fat (grams)	17	6
% calories from fat	50	27
Cholesterol (mg)	33	0

Crust

¾ cup graham cracker crumbs

⅓ cup nugget cereal (such as Grape-Nuts)

¼ cup chopped nuts, toasted

2 tablespoons packed light brown sugar

3 tablespoons apricot jam, melted

Filling

1 quart fat-free vanilla ice cream or frozen yogurt

⅓ cup natural-style chunky peanut butter

½ cup light corn syrup

⅓ cup chopped nuts, toasted

Preheat the oven to 350° F. Lightly coat a 9x9x2-inch baking pan with nonstick vegetable-oil spray.

To make the crust: In a small bowl, stir together the graham cracker crumbs, nugget cereal, chopped nuts, and brown sugar. Drizzle in the melted jam. Using a fork, stir until well mixed. Transfer the crumb mixture to the prepared pan. Using the back of large spoon or wet fingertips, press the crumb mixture firmly on the bottom of the pan. Bake 5 to 7 minutes, or until light brown. Place the pan in the freezer while preparing the ice-cream filling.

To make the filling: In a medium bowl, stir ice cream with a wooden spoon to soften; set aside. In a small bowl, stir together the peanut butter and the corn syrup. Spoon half of the ice cream over the crust. Spread the peanut butter mixture over the ice cream layer. Carefully spread the remaining ice cream over the peanut butter layer. Sprinkle with the nuts. Cover and freeze 6 to 24 hours.

Before serving, let stand at room temperature for 5 minutes. Cut into 16 squares.

Grasshopper Mint Pie

Serves 8

❈❈❈❈❈

This pie is refreshing and a cinch to make! It's a great dessert to serve for a party because you can make it ahead of time and it stores well in the freezer.

How fat and calories were lowered:

☛ Used a low-fat chocolate crust

☛ Replaced whipping cream with a combination of fat-free ricotta cheese and light whipped topping.

Nutrition Scorecard
(per serving)

	Before	After
Calories	507	260
Fat (grams)	34	5
% calories from fat	63	17
Cholesterol (mg)	89	3

---

1 recipe Chocolate Cookie Crust (page 60)

1 (7½-ounce) jar marshmallow creme

1 cup fat-free ricotta

2 tablespoons crème de cacao

¼ cup crème de menthe

1½ cups thawed frozen light whipped topping

1 tablespoon fat-free fudge topping

Chill the chocolate crust.

Meanwhile, in a medium bowl, combine the marshmallow creme, fat-free ricotta, and crème de cacao and beat with an electric mixer on low speed until smooth. Add the crème de menthe and beat until blended. Fold in the light whipped topping. Spoon the filling into the chilled crust. Freeze until firm (at least 5 hours). Just before serving, drizzle the fat-free fudge topping over the pie.

Caramel Pecan Ice Cream Pie

Serves 12

U niversally declared the best of my ice cream desserts. It's great to make ahead and serve for a party. Don't even think about using a ready-made pie crust. The pecan crust enhances and complements the caramel flavor. Tip: To melt jam, microwave 10 to 15 seconds.

How fat and calories were lowered:

- In the crust: reduced the amount of pecans, eliminated butter, and reduced the amount of sugar

- In the sauce: replaced butter with light butter and used less; replaced whipping cream with a combination of evaporated skim milk and cornstarch

- Replaced ice cream with fat-free ice cream

Nutrition Scorecard
(per serving)

	Before	After
Calories	782	477
Fat (grams)	48	7.5
% calories from fat	54	14
Cholesterol (mg)	124	12

Pecan Cookie Crust

30 vanilla wafers, reduced fat

1/2 cup chopped pecans, toasted

1/4 cup brown sugar

3 tablespoons apricot jam, melted

Caramel Sauce

4 tablespoons light butter

3/4 cup evaporated skim milk

1 tablespoon cornstarch

1 1/2 cups packed light brown sugar

1/2 teaspoon vanilla extract

Filling

1/2 gallon fat-free butter pecan or praline ice cream or frozen yogurt, softened slightly

12 pecan halves, toasted (optional)

To make the crust: Preheat the oven to 350° F. Lightly coat 10-inch round spring-form pan with nonstick vegetable-oil spray; set aside.

Place the vanilla wafers in a food processor or blender and pulse until crumblike. Add the toasted pecans and brown sugar and pulse until mixed thoroughly. Transfer to medium bowl and drizzle in the melted jam. Using a fork, stir until well mixed. Transfer the crumb mixture to the prepared pan. Using the back of a large spoon or wet fingertips, press the crumb mixture firmly on the bottom and 1/2 inch up the sides of prepared pan. Bake until the crust begins to brown, about 10 to 12 minutes. Let crust cool completely.

To make the caramel sauce: Melt the light butter in a medium saucepan over medium heat. In a custard cup or small dish, combine 2 tablespoons of the milk with the cornstarch and stir until smooth. Add the remaining milk, the cornstarch mixture, and the 1½ cups brown sugar to the melted butter, stirring constantly over medium heat until the mixture comes to a boil. Remove from the heat and mix in the vanilla. Let sauce cool completely, stirring occasionally.

To assemble: Spoon the fat-free ice cream into the crust, pressing to compact. Pour about ½ cup of sauce over the ice cream. Using the tip of a small knife, swirl the sauce and the top of the ice cream, creating marbled pattern. Cover the pie and freeze 12 hours. Cover the remaining sauce and refrigerate.

Run a small sharp knife around the pan sides to loosen the pie. Release the pan sides. Let the pie stand 5 minutes. Arrange the pecans halves decoratively on the pie, if using. Cut the pie into wedges. Serve with remaining caramel sauce.

Sugar Does Not Cause Hyperactivity

Contrary to popular belief, sugar does not cause children to be hyperactive. Researchers reviewed 23 sugar studies from 1982 to 1994. They found no evidence that sugar causes hyperactivity. But interestingly, they found that the parents' beliefs and expectations can have a significant effect. For example, it's quite typical for kids to be excited for special events, such as birthday parties, where extra sugar is likely to be eaten. The association with the sugary treats and excited behavior can erroneously perpetuate a parent's belief that sugar triggers hyperactivity.

Source: M. L. Wolraich, et al., *The Journal of the American Medical Association* 274(1995):1617.

Strawberry Yogurt Pie

Serves 6

❧❧❧❧❧

I couldn't believe how much fat was in the original version of this healthy-sounding pie. With a little fat cutting, it now lives up to its healthy image. The glazed fresh strawberries make this especially appealing in the summer.

How fat and calories were lowered:

☛ Used reduced fat crust

☛ Replaced cream cheese with reduced fat version

Nutrition Scorecard (per serving)		
	Before	*After*
Calories	332	275
Fat (grams)	20	8
% calories from fat	55	27
Cholesterol (mg)	41	14

8 ounces tub-style light cream cheese

8 ounces nonfat strawberry yogurt

1 tablespoon honey

1 teaspoon vanilla extract

1 (¼-ounce) envelope unflavored gelatin

¾ cup water, divided use

1 graham cracker pie crust (see page 38)

1 cup strawberries, washed, hulled, and thinly sliced

¼ cup strawberry jam, melted

In a medium bowl, beat the light cream cheese until smooth. Stir in the yogurt, honey, and vanilla. Sprinkle the gelatin over ¼ cup of the water in a saucepan; let soften 1 minute. Stir over low heat to dissolve the gelatin. Stir the gelatin mixture and the remaining ½ cup water into the cheese mixture. Spread evenly into prepared crust. Cover and refrigerate overnight.

To serve, top pie with strawberries. Using a pastry brush or spoon, glaze the strawberries with the melted jam.

Chocolate Chip Almond Coconut
    Cookies

Chocolate Meringue Cookies

Chocolate Turtle Pecan
    Cookies

Three-Layer Fudge
    Bars

Grasshopper Mint Pie

Tropical Shake

Frozen Raspberry Ribbon Pie

Red-White-and-Blueberry Mold

Serves 10

❧❧❧❧❧

This gelatin dessert looks spectacular any time of the year and makes for a patriotic treat.

How fat and calories were lowered:

☞ Used nonfat milk instead of whole milk

☞ Replaced cream cheese with a combination of light tub-style and fat-free cream cheeses

☞ Replaced whole eggs with egg substitute

1 (3-ounce) package strawberry-flavor gelatin

¾ cup boiling water

¾ cup cold water

1 pint strawberries, sliced

1 pint blueberries

½ cup sugar

1 (¼-ounce) envelope unflavored gelatin

½ cup nonfat milk

4 ounces frozen egg substitute, thawed

8 ounces tub-style light cream cheese

8 ounces fat-free cream cheese

1 teaspoon almond extract

In a medium bowl, stir the strawberry gelatin with the ¾ cup boiling water until the gelatin is completely dissolved. Stir in the ¾ cup cold water. Pour a ⅛-inch layer of strawberry gelatin into a 6-cup gelatin mold; refrigerate until almost set, about 10 minutes.

Arrange a few strawberry slices and some blueberries on the gelatin layer to make a pretty design; refrigerate until set.

Refrigerate the remaining strawberry-flavor gelatin until it mounds when dropped from a spoon. Fold in ¼ cup of the blueberries and 1 cup of the strawberries (reserving remaining berries for garnish). Spoon this gelatin-and-fruit mixture over the gelatin layer in the mold.

Meanwhile, mix the sugar, unflavored gelatin, and milk in a medium saucepan. Cook over medium-low heat, stirring constantly, until the gelatin is dissolved and the mixture coats the back of a spoon (do not boil). Remove the saucepan from the heat.

In a small bowl beat the egg substitute with an electric mixer at high speed until thickened and foamy, about 5 minutes. In a large bowl, beat the light and fat-free cream cheeses and almond extract with mixer at low speed until smooth. Gradually beat in the unflavored gelatin mixture; add the beaten egg substitute. Pour the cream cheese mixture over the strawberry layer in the mold. Cover and refrigerate until set, about 4 hours.

To serve, unmold the gelatin onto a platter. Garnish the mold with the reserved berries.

Say No to Raw Eggs

Recipes that use raw eggs in the finished product are very risky (too risky) to eat. In fact, the U.S. Department of Agriculture does not recommend eating raw or undercooked egg yolks or whites, or products containing them. This is because eggs have been implicated in a number of cases of foodborne illness. The culprit: a bacterium called *Salmonella enteritidis*. The good news is that cooking destroys the bacteria.

Safe at the dessert plate.

1. To make safe favorite recipes that call for raw eggs in the finished product, use powdered egg whites. They are pasteurized, which destroys the salmonella bacterium. Here are two brands that are only a toll-free call away:
   Just Whites by Deb-El Foods at 800-421-Eggs or
   Powdered Egg Whites by Ener-G Foods at 1-800-331-5222.

2. Egg substitute can also be used in recipes, because it is pasteurized, but it won't whip up into a foam or meringue.

3. Bake all meringue-topped desserts at 350° F for at least 15 minutes.

4. Buy only eggs that have been refrigerated, never those sitting out at room temperature.

5. Proper storage: Fresh shell eggs can be kept safely in the refrigerator 3 to 5 weeks from the date of purchase, not from the date on the carton.

6. If you have leftover egg whites from a recipe, refrigerate them in a tightly closed container, and you can store them for up to 4 days.

7. Avoid keeping eggs out of the refrigerator for more than 2 hours, including time for preparing (but not cooking).

8. Have more questions? Call USDA's hotline at 1-800-535-4555.

Source: USDA, *Food News for Consumers* 9(1992):13.

Raspberry Thrill Pie

Serves 8

❧❧❧❧❧

This deep-red pie was demolished lickety split by my family before I could get it out the door for friends to taste!

How fat and calories were lowered:

☞ Replaced cream cheese with fat-free cream cheese

☞ Replaced whipped cream with light whipped topping

☞ Used reduced fat graham cracker crust

Nutrition Scorecard (per serving)		
	Before	After
Calories	281	206
Fat (grams)	14	5
% calories from fat	43	22
Cholesterol (mg)	25	5

1 (0.6-ounce) package sugar-free gelatin, raspberry flavor

1 cup boiling water

8 ounces fat-free cream cheese, softened

1½ cups frozen light whipped topping, thawed

1¾ cup fresh or frozen dry-pack raspberries, partially thawed

1 graham cracker crust (see page 38), cooled

Combine the gelatin and water in a large bowl. Stir until dissolved. In a medium bowl, beat the cream cheese until smooth; fold in the whipped topping. Fold the cream cheese mixture into the gelatin until blended. Fold the berries into the gelatin mixture. Spoon the filling into the prepared pie crust. Refrigerate at least 4 hours before serving.

Cherry Delicious

Serves 8

❧❧❧❧❧

This is a variation of a family favorite that I've enjoyed since childhood. It's quick and simple to make.

How fat and calories were lowered:

☞ Replaced cream cheese with a combination of light and fat-free cream cheese

☞ Replaced whipping cream with vanilla pudding

☞ Used light cherry filling

<table>
<tr><td colspan="3">**Nutrition Scorecard**
(per serving)</td></tr>
<tr><td></td><td>*Before*</td><td>*After*</td></tr>
<tr><td>Calories</td><td>414</td><td>286</td></tr>
<tr><td>Fat (grams)</td><td>22</td><td>6</td></tr>
<tr><td>% calories from fat</td><td>51</td><td>21</td></tr>
<tr><td>Cholesterol (mg)</td><td>31</td><td>16</td></tr>
</table>

8 ounces light cream cheese, softened

8 ounces fat-free cream cheese, softened

1 (1-ounce) package sugar-free instant
   vanilla pudding

1¼ cup cold nonfat milk

1 (20-ounce) can light cherry filling

1 graham cracker crust (see page 38),
   cooled

In a mixing bowl, beat together light and fat-free cream cheeses until smooth. Add instant pudding and milk and beat until mixture is smooth and begins to thicken, at least 2 minutes. Pour into the prepared crust. Top with the cherry filling. Refrigerate at least 3 hours. (Tastes even better when chilled overnight.)

Zesty Lemon Sherbet

Makes 1½ quarts; 8 ¾-cup servings

❧❧❧❧❧

$\mathcal{S}$uch a refreshing treat on a hot summer day, and you don't even need an ice-cream maker. *Tip: Be sure to zest the lemons before you juice them.* How fat and calories were lowered:

🖝 Replaced the cream with a combination of evaporated skim milk and beaten egg substitute

🖝 Used nonfat milk in place of regular milk

🖝 Slightly reduced the amount of sugar

Nutrition Scorecard (per serving)		
	Before	After
Calories	270	153
Fat (grams)	9	0
% calories from fat	29	<1
Cholesterol (mg)	31	0

1⅓ cups sugar	½ cup evaporated skim milk
1 (¼-ounce) envelope unflavored gelatin	½ cup nonfat milk
2½ cups water	¾ cup fresh lemon juice
4 ounces frozen egg substitute, thawed	2 teaspoons finely grated lemon zest

In a medium saucepan, mix the sugar and gelatin; add the water. Cook and stir until sugar and gelatin dissolve (do not boil). Remove from heat.

In a large mixing bowl, beat the egg substitute until thick and foamy (about 5 minutes). Add evaporated skim milk and nonfat milk; beat well until thoroughly blended. Beat in the lemon juice and zest (mixture may look curdled). Slowly drizzle in the gelatin mixture while beating at medium speed. Transfer to a 9x9x2-inch baking pan. Cover and freeze 2 to 3 hours, or until almost firm. (Or after mixing ingredients, transfer to a 4-quart ice cream maker and proceed according to the manufacturer's directions. Omit remaining steps.)

Break the frozen mixture into small chunks and transfer to a chilled bowl. Beat with an electric mixer until smooth but not melted. Return to pan. Cover and freeze until firm, about 1 hour.

Cool Lemon Slush

Transfer lemon mixture to ice trays, freeze. Place in blender or food processor. Puree until smooth. Pour into 8 chilled glasses and serve.

Fluffy Mocha Pie

Serves 8

❈ ❈ ❈ ❈ ❈

O*ne of my favorites to serve at parties, elegant and yet easy to prepare ahead of time.*

How fat and calories were lowered:

☞ Used a combination of light whipped topping and instant pudding instead of whipping cream

☞ Added gelatin for body

☞ Used fat-free fudge topping instead of chocolate chips and enhanced flavor with a coffee liqueur

☞ Used a lower-fat chocolate cookie crust

Nutrition Scorecard
(per serving)

	Before	After
Calories	479	205
Fat (grams)	30	7
% calories from fat	59	29
Cholesterol (mg)	71	<1

1 ½ cups nonfat milk, divided use

1 (¼-ounce) envelope of unflavored gelatin

1 tablespoon instant coffee granules

1 (1-ounce) package of sugar-free instant vanilla pudding mix

1 (8-ounce) tub thawed frozen light whipped topping

1 Chocolate Cookie Crust (page 60)

⅓ cup fat-free fudge topping

1 tablespoon coffee liqueur

Put ½ cup of the milk in a small saucepan and sprinkle the gelatin over the milk to soften, about 1 minute. Cook over medium low heat to dissolve; do not boil. Remove from the heat.

In a medium bowl, dissolve the coffee with the remaining milk. Add the pudding mix and beat with an electric mixer on medium speed for 60 seconds. Gradually add the gelatin mixture and beat for an additional 60 seconds. Fold in the whipped topping. Transfer to the prepared cookie pie crust. Combine fudge topping with coffee liqueur and drizzle on top of filled pie. Using the tip of a knife, create a marbleized effect by swirling back and forth. Refrigerate for 4 hours.

Rainbow Freeze

Serves 16

✄ ✄ ✄ ✄ ✄

This five-layer dessert derives its unique texture from the coconut and walnuts.

How fat and calories were lowered:

☞ Used a combination of evaporated skim milk and light nondairy topping instead of whipping cream

☞ Substituted a combination of coconut and graham cracker crumbs for macaroons

☞ Reduced the amount of nuts

Nutrition Scorecard
(per serving)

	Before	After
Calories	363	245
Fat (grams)	21	8
% calories from fat	51	29
Cholesterol (mg)	47	7

½ cup plus 2 tablespoons chilled evaporated skim milk

1 teaspoon unflavored gelatin

3 tablespoons boiling water

⅓ cup light corn syrup

1½ cups frozen light whipped topping, thawed

1 cup shredded coconut

¾ cup graham cracker crumbs

⅔ cup chopped walnuts

1 pint orange sherbet, softened

1 pint lime sherbet, softened

1 pint raspberry sherbet, softened

Lightly coat a 12-cup Bundt pan or 12-cup mold with nonstick vegetable-oil spray.

Put the 2 tablespoons milk in a medium bowl, sprinkle the gelatin over the milk, and let stand at least 2 minutes. Add the boiling water and stir until gelatin dissolves. Add the remaining ½ cup milk. Using an electric mixer at highest speed, blend until opaque and fluffy (volume will double in size). Gradually drizzle in the corn syrup while mixing. Fold in the light whipped topping. Fold in the coconut, graham cracker crumbs, and walnuts. Spread *half* of the whipped milk mixture in the prepared mold. Freeze until firm. Refrigerate the remaining mixture.

Layer the orange, lime, and raspberry sherbets on top of the frozen whipped milk layer in the mold. As necessary, place the mold in the freezer between adding layers to prevent the layers from running together. Top with the remaining whipped milk mixture. Cover and freeze at least 6 hours. To unmold, briefly dip the mold in *hot* water and invert onto a platter.

Frozen Peanut Butter Fudge Pie

Serves 8

❧❧❧❧❧

This is a great pie to make ahead for parties, a real crowd pleaser.
How fat and calories were lowered:

- Replaced cream cheese with a combination of light and
  fat-free cream cheese

- Used a combination of evaporated skim milk and gelatin
  instead of a nondairy topping

- Reduced the amount of peanut butter chips

Nutrition Scorecard
(per serving)

	Before	After
Calories	693	338
Fat (grams)	39	8
% calories from fat	52	21
Cholesterol (mg)	13	5

1 prepared graham cracker pie crust

  (see page 38)

Peanut Butter Filling

¼ cup tub-style light cream cheese

¼ cup tub-style fat-free cream cheese

¼ cup chunky natural-style peanut butter

¾ cup powdered sugar

¼ cup evaporated skim milk

½ cup fat-free fudge topping

Topping

½ cup plus 2 tablespoons chilled evaporated skim milk

1 teaspoon unflavored gelatin

3 tablespoons boiling water

1 teaspoon vanilla extract

⅓ cup light corn syrup

3 tablespoons peanut butter chips

To make the filling: In a small bowl, cream together the light and fat-free cream
cheeses, peanut butter, sugar, and evaporated skim milk. Pour into the prepared pie crust.

To make the topping: Put 2 tablespoons of the chilled evaporated skim milk in a
large bowl and sprinkle the gelatin over the top. Add the boiling water to the gelatin mixture and mix well until gelatin is dissolved. Add the remaining ½ cup chilled evaporated
skim milk and vanilla to the dissolved gelatin mixture. Using an electric mixer, beat until
foamy and opaque. Gradually drizzle in the corn syrup while beating until soft peaks form.
Pour onto pie filling. Put in freezer.

Meanwhile, in a food processor or blender, grind peanut butter chips until they resem-
ble coarse bread crumbs and sprinkle over the pie topping. Freeze until firm. Before slicing
and serving, let stand 15 minutes in the refrigerator.

Mile-High Sundae Pie

Serves 12

❈❈❈❈❈

What a winner this impressive-looking dessert is, and it's a cinch to make.

How fat and calories were lowered:

☞ Used a lower-fat chocolate cookie pie crust

☞ Reduced the amount of nuts

☞ Used crumbled cookies instead of toffee candy

☞ Replaced regular ice cream with premium fat-free ice cream

Nutrition Scorecard
(per serving)

	Before	After
Calories	671	473
Fat (grams)	38	3
% calories from fat	51	6
Cholesterol (mg)	114	0

1 recipe Chocolate Cookie Crust (page 60), made as directed below

1 quart premium fat-free coffee ice cream or frozen yogurt, softened

1 quart premium fat-free chocolate ice cream or frozen yogurt

1 cup fat-free fudge topping

1 quart premium fat-free vanilla ice cream or frozen yogurt

3 tablespoons chopped almonds

6 chocolate wafer cookies, crumbled

Prepare cookie crust ingredients as directed, except press into the bottom of a 9-inch springform pan. Spread coffee ice cream onto cooled crust. Freeze until firm, about 1 hour. Meanwhile, refrigerate chocolate ice cream to soften slightly, 30 minutes.

Spread ½ cup fudge topping over firm coffee layer. Quickly spread the chocolate ice cream over the fudge layer. Freeze 1 hour. Layer with remaining fudge topping.

Soften the vanilla ice cream as done above. Quickly spread over the fudge topping layer. Sprinkle with chopped almonds and chocolate cookie crumbs. Cover and freeze. Before slicing and serving, let stand 15 minutes in the refrigerator.

Frozen Raspberry Ribbon Pie

Serves 8

⌘ ⌘ ⌘ ⌘ ⌘

You get double the raspberry flavor with two ribbon layers of this berry puree.

How fat and calories were lowered:

- Used a low-fat cookie crust
- Eliminated butter from raspberry filling and replaced it with corn syrup
- Used fat-free ice cream

Nutrition Scorecard
(per serving)

	Before	After
Calories	581	349
Fat (grams)	33	3
% calories from fat	51	8
Cholesterol (mg)	68	0

1 recipe Chocolate Cookie Crust (page 60)

2 cups fresh raspberries

1 tablespoon cornstarch

⅓ cup light corn syrup

2 pints vanilla fat-free ice cream or frozen yogurt, softened

Meringue Topping

3 tablespoons powdered egg whites (see page 44)

½ cup warm water

⅓ cup sugar

½ teaspoon vanilla extract

Chill the chocolate cookie crust. Meanwhile, for the filling, puree the raspberries in a food processor or blender, then strain through a fine sieve into a small saucepan. Combine a tablespoonful of the raspberry sauce with the cornstarch and stir until smooth and pasty; add cornstarch mixture and corn syrup. Cook and stir over medium heat until bubbly. Remove from heat; chill.

Quickly spread 1 pint of softened fat-free ice cream evenly over chilled crust. Cover with half of the thickened raspberry puree. Repeat layering with the remaining ice cream and raspberry puree. Freeze 30 minutes. Cover the pie and freeze overnight.

Preheat oven to 450° F. In a large bowl add the powdered egg whites to the warm water. Stir gently until dissolved, about 3 minutes. With an electric mixer on high setting, beat until soft peaks form. Gradually beat in the sugar and the vanilla and continue to beat until stiff peaks form. Unwrap frozen pie. With a spatula, spread the meringue completely over the top of the pie, mounding more meringue in center. Bake until the topping is browned, about 2 minutes. Immediately place in the freezer and freeze at least 1 hour.

Tropical Shake

Makes 2 cups; serves 2

❈❈❈❈❈

This drink is so remarkably creamy, it's hard to believe it's fat-free. The fresh fruit and nonfat milk make it a wholesome snack or mini meal.

How fat and calories were lowered:

☛ Replaced coconut milk with a combination of nonfat milk and coconut extract

☛ Replaced ice cream with nonfat frozen vanilla yogurt

Nutrition Scorecard
(per serving)

	Before	After
Calories	412	267
Fat (grams)	25	0
% calories from fat	50	0
Cholesterol (mg)	44	1

1 large mango, peeled, pitted, and cut into 1-inch chunks (about 1¼ cups)

⅓ cup fresh lime juice

½ cup nonfat milk

½ teaspoon coconut extract

1½ cups nonfat frozen vanilla yogurt

Combine mango chunks and lime juice in blender and whirl until smooth. Mix in the milk and coconut extract. Add the frozen yogurt and blend to desired consistency.

Fresh Strawberry Shake

Serves 2

✄✄✄✄✄

California may not have distinct seasons, but we eagerly await the arrival of fresh strawberries at the roadside stands that pop up annually with each new harvest. My family always inaugurates strawberry season by making these delicious milkshakes, sans fat.

How fat and calories were lowered:

☞ Used fat-free ice cream instead of regular

☞ Used nonfat milk instead of whole milk

Nutrition Scorecard (per serving)		
	Before	*After*
Calories	366	296
Fat (grams)	18	0
% calories from fat	42	2
Cholesterol (mg)	70	0

1 pint fresh strawberries, washed and hulled

⅔ cup nonfat milk

½ teaspoon vanilla extract

2 cups fat-free vanilla ice cream or frozen yogurt

In a blender, combine the strawberries, milk, and vanilla and blend until smooth. Gradually add the ice cream. Blend until the shake reaches the desired consistency.

Hearty Pies,

Tarts,

and Crisps

Key Lime Pie

Serves 8

❊❊❊❊❊

*T*his zesty pie was made even healthier by replacing two of the egg yolks with creamy yogurt cheese.

How fat and calories were lowered:

☛ Replaced pie crust with lower-fat version

☛ Eliminated two egg yolks

☛ Used fat-free sweetened condensed milk

Nutrition Scorecard
(per serving)

	Before	After
Calories	302	278
Fat (grams)	14	2
% calories from fat	41	6
Cholesterol (mg)	97	27

1 prepared graham cracker crust
    (see page 38)

Lime Yogurt Cheese

1 cup nonfat plain yogurt

1½ teaspoons finely grated lime zest,
    divided use

Lime Filling

1 egg

1 (14-ounce) can fat-free sweetened
    condensed milk

1½ teaspoons finely grated lime zest

⅓ cup fresh lime juice

To make the lime yogurt cheese: Combine the yogurt with 1½ teaspoons of the lime zest. Line a strainer with a double layer of cheesecloth or a coffee filter. Place the strainer over a bowl to allow the whey from the yogurt to drip into it. Spoon the yogurt mixture into the strainer; drain in the refrigerator until thickened, at least 4 hours or overnight. Discard accumulated whey in bowl and reserve cheese curds in strainer for use in recipe.

To make the lime filling: In a medium bowl, beat the egg until thick and lemon-colored. Stir in the condensed milk, remaining lime zest, and yogurt cheese. Gradually add the lime juice, beating at low speed, just until combined. Do not overbeat. Spoon mixture into the prepared graham cracker shell. Bake 25 to 30 minutes. Let cool on a wire rack. Cover and chill to store.

Peach Melba Tart

Serves 10

✄✄✄✄✄

This is a family favorite that I'm always proud to serve to guests. The peach glaze is a cinch to make. Tip: If you don't have a tart pan, a 10-inch springform pan works just as well.

How fat and calories were lowered:

☞ Used a lowfat pastry shell

☞ Replaced regular cream cheese with a combination of light and fat-free cream cheese

Nutrition Scorecard
(per serving)

	Before	After
Calories	559	195
Fat (grams)	26	6
% calories from fat	42	25
Cholesterol (mg)	82	8

1 Tart Pastry shell *(page 58)*, cooled

Filling

8 ounces fat-free cream cheese

4 ounces tub-style light cream cheese

½ cup powdered sugar

1 teaspoon vanilla extract

Peach Glaze

⅓ cup granulated sugar

1 tablespoon cornstarch

¾ cup peach nectar

Fruits

2 kiwis, peeled and thinly sliced

1 peach, peeled, pitted, and thinly sliced

1 (6-ounce) basket fresh raspberries

In a small bowl, beat together the cream cheeses, powdered sugar, and vanilla. Spread the mixture on the cooled crust. Chill.

In small saucepan, stir together the granulated sugar and cornstarch. Stir in the peach nectar. Cook and stir over medium heat until the mixture begins to bubble. Cook and stir for 1 minute more. Remove from heat and let cool at least 5 minutes.

Using a clean pastry brush, apply a thin layer of glaze over the cream cheese filling. Add kiwi slices and apply another thin layer of glaze. Add peach slices and glaze again. Top with raspberries and remaining glaze.

Tart Pastry

Serves 10

❧❧❧❧❧

I love how the lemon zest accents this cookielike pastry. It's easy to make because you don't have to roll out the dough. Glazing the shell with egg white prevents the crust from getting soggy.

How fat and calories were lowered:

☞ Replaced lard with a combination of buttermilk and canola oil

☞ Added nuts and lemon zest for enhanced flavor and texture

Nutrition Scorecard *(per serving)*		
	Before	*After*
Calories	145	98
Fat (grams)	9	3
% calories from fat	54	30
Cholesterol (mg)	6	0

½ cup whole-wheat flour

½ cup all-purpose flour

¼ cup finely chopped walnuts

3 tablespoons sugar

1 teaspoon finely grated lemon zest

⅓ cup buttermilk

1 tablespoon canola oil

½ egg white, slightly beaten

Preheat the oven to 375° F. Lightly coat a 9-inch fluted tart pan (with removable bottom) with nonstick vegetable-oil spray.

In a medium bowl, combine the flours, walnuts, sugar, and lemon zest. In a small bowl, whisk together the buttermilk and oil until well blended; add to the flour mixture. Blend with a fork or pastry cutter until the mixture resembles coarse crumbs. Press the dough into the prepared pan. Using a pastry brush or rubber spatula, glaze crust with egg white. Bake 12 to 15 minutes, until the edges begin to brown slightly.

Desserts are one of the top five major contributors of total fat in the diet for children and teens.

Source: *Journal of the American Dietetic Association* 10(1995):1127.

❧❧❧❧❧

Peach Melba Tart

Lemon Meringue Pie

✣

Fat–Free Apricot Fool

Chocolate Fudge Pudding

Orange Cream Cheese Bavarian

White Chocolate Mousse with

Raspberry Compote

One-Crust Pastry

Serves 8

⋈ ⋈ ⋈ ⋈ ⋈

Pie crust is the chief fatty culprit in most pies. This recipe is substantially lower in fat and half the calories than a traditional butter crust. If
you want a fat-free pastry, try the phyllo pastry crust on page 70.

How fat and calories were lowered:

🖙 Used light butter in place of butter and grated it for a better texture. Also, used a smaller quantity. Grating the butter allows for a more thorough incorporation without
overmixing. Tip: Keep a stick of light butter in the
freezer—that makes it even easier to shred.

Nutrition Scorecard		
(per serving)		
	Before	After
Calories	199	105
Fat (grams)	12	4
% calories from fat	53	37
Cholesterol (mg)	31	11

6 tablespoons cold light butter

¾ cup all-purpose flour

¼ cup whole-wheat flour

2 tablespoons sugar

⅛ teaspoon salt

¼ cup ice water

1 teaspoon white distilled vinegar

Generously coat a 9-inch pie plate with nonstick vegetable-oil spray.

Using a grater, shred the chilled light butter; place the light butter in the freezer while
you do the next step.

In a large bowl, combine the flours, the sugar, and the salt. Cut in the light butter with a
pastry knife or 2 knives. Combine the water and vinegar in a measuring cup and sprinkle
over the flour mixture. Toss the pastry with a fork until it just comes together. Gather the
pastry together in a ball and flatten the ball into a disk. Place the dough between sheets of
wax paper. Roll dough from center to edges, forming a circle about 12 inches in diameter.
Wrap the pastry around the rolling pin and unroll it onto the prepared pie plate. Ease the
pastry into the pie plate, being careful not to stretch it. Trim it to 1/2 inch beyond the edge
of the pie plate; fold the extra pastry under.

For filled one-crust pie: Fill and bake as directed in recipe.

For baked one-crust pie shell (unfilled): Prick the bottom and sides of the pastry all over with a fork. Bake at 450° F. for 9 to 12 minutes, until golden. Let cool on a wire
rack. Continue as directed in recipe.

Chocolate Cookie Crust

Serves 8

✂ ✂ ✂ ✂ ✂

I *added a little bit of instant coffee to intensify the chocolate flavor. It also helped to "glue" the crumbs together without margarine.*

How fat and calories were lowered:

☛ Replaced margarine with an egg white and concentrated instant coffee

☛ Eliminated the sugar (chocolate cookies are already sweet enough!)

Nutrition Scorecard *(per serving)*		
	Before	*After*
Calories	149	82
Fat *(grams)*	9	3
% calories from fat	51	32
Cholesterol *(mg)*	0	0

½ *teaspoon water*

1 *teaspoon instant coffee granules*

1 *egg white*

1 *cup chocolate cookie crumbs*

Preheat the oven to 375° F. Lightly coat a 9-inch pie plate with nonstick vegetable-oil spray.

In a small bowl, combine the water and instant coffee; mix well. Stir in the egg white. In a large bowl, combine the cookie crumbs and the egg white mixture, stirring with a fork until crumbly. Using the back of a large spoon, press the crumb mixture onto the bottom of the prepared pie plate. Bake 8 to 10 minutes.

Boysenberry Sour Cream Crumb

Serves 8

❦❦❦❦❦

I adore boysenberries, and this is one of my favorite desserts to make with them. It's so rich-tasting, yet it has virtually no fat. Frozen berries also work surprisingly well in this dish.

How fat and calories were lowered:

- Omitted butter in bread crumb mixture
- Used fat-free sour cream instead of regular sour cream
- Eliminated pastry crust

Nutrition Scorecard
(per serving)

	Before	After
Calories	413	221
Fat (grams)	15	0
% calories from fat	33	2
Cholesterol (mg)	17	0

Filling

4 cups fresh or frozen boysenberries,
    slightly thawed

½ cup sugar

¼ cup all-purpose flour

Topping

1 cup fat-free sour cream (containing no
    gelatin)

¾ cup sugar

3 tablespoons all-purpose flour

¼ cup fine, dry bread crumbs

2 tablespoons sugar

Preheat the oven to 375° F.

In a large bowl, lightly toss together the boysenberries, the ½ cup sugar, and the ¼ cup flour. Place in a 9-inch pie plate. In a small bowl, stir together fat-free sour cream, the ¾ cup sugar, and the 3 tablespoons flour. Spread the mixture evenly over the berries. In a small bowl, stir together the bread crumbs and 2 tablespoons sugar. Sprinkle the bread crumb mixture on top of the sour cream mixture. Bake for 35 to 40 minutes, until bubbly and golden. Let cool to room temperature on a wire rack. Serve in bowls.

Cherry Crunch

Serves 8

❧❧❧❧❧

Ihe crunchy topping is absolutely delicious. I incorporated whole-wheat flour to increase the nutritional value of this tasty dessert.

How fat and calories were lowered:

☛ Used buttermilk in place of butter

☛ Reduced the amount of walnuts

<table>
<tr><th colspan="3">Nutrition Scorecard
(per serving)</th></tr>
<tr><th></th><th>Before</th><th>After</th></tr>
<tr><td>Calories</td><td>407</td><td>291</td></tr>
<tr><td>Fat (grams)</td><td>17</td><td>4</td></tr>
<tr><td>% calories from fat</td><td>36</td><td>12</td></tr>
<tr><td>Cholesterol (mg)</td><td>31</td><td>0</td></tr>
</table>

2 cups drained and pitted canned sweet cherries (reserve ½ cup cherry juice)

2 tablespoons sugar

1½ tablespoons instant tapioca

½ teaspoon almond extract

½ cup whole-wheat flour

½ cup all-purpose flour

¼ teaspoon baking powder

¼ teaspoon baking soda

1 cup packed light brown sugar

1 cup old-fashioned oats

⅓ cup chopped walnuts

⅓ cup buttermilk

Preheat the oven to 350° F.

Place the cherries in 9x9x2-inch pan; set aside.

In a small bowl, mix ½ cup of the reserved cherry juice with the 2 tablespoons sugar, the tapioca, and the almond extract. Set aside for 15 minutes. Pour the cherry juice mixture over the cherries.

In a medium bowl, combine the whole-wheat flour, all-purpose flour, baking powder, baking soda, and brown sugar. Stir in the oats and walnuts. Drizzle in the buttermilk, using a fork to stir. Mix until crumbly. Spoon flour mixture over cherries. Bake 20 to 25 minutes, or until bubbly and golden brown.

Apple Crisp

Serves 6

✄✄ ✄✄ ✄✄

Any apple will do in this dish, but I am partial to the mellow sweetness of Golden Delicious apples.

How fat and calories were lowered:

☞ Reduced the amount of pecans

☞ Replaced the butter in the topping with buttermilk

Nutrition Scorecard
(per serving)

	Before	After
Calories	452	334
Fat (grams)	19	5
% calories from fat	26	14
Cholesterol (mg)	37	0

Filling

5 to 6 medium apples, peeled, cored, and
    thinly sliced (7½ cups)

2 tablespoons fresh lemon juice or fresh
    orange juice

⅓ cup sugar

¼ cup all-purpose flour

½ teaspoon cinnamon

Topping

⅓ cup whole-wheat flour

¼ cup all-purpose flour

⅔ cup packed light brown sugar

⅓ cup chopped pecans

½ teaspoon cinnamon

¼ cup old-fashioned oats

¼ cup buttermilk

Preheat the oven to 350° F. Lightly coat an 8-inch square pan with nonstick vegetable-oil spray.

To make the filling: In a large bowl, toss together the sliced apples and lemon juice. In a small bowl, combine the ⅓ cup sugar, the ¼ cup flour, and the cinnamon. Sprinkle the flour mixture over the apples and toss well. Place the apples in the prepared pan.

To make the topping: In a medium bowl, combine both flours and the brown sugar, pecans, cinnamon, and oats. Using an electric mixer on low speed, slowly drizzle in the buttermilk and beat until well mixed. Spread the topping evenly over the apples.

Bake 35 to 40 minutes, until bubbly and golden.

Lemon Meringue Pie

Serves 8

✄ ✄ ✄ ✄ ✄

My sister and I both had immense cravings for lemon meringue pie while pregnant. This is the best lemon meringue pie I've tasted—and as luck would have it, my sister was pregnant when she sampled this. She gave it two thumbs up (one from the baby!). Tip: Remember to zest those lemons before you squeeze out the juice.

How fat and calories were lowered:

☛ Eliminated two egg yolks and replaced them with a little extra cornstarch

☛ Eliminated the butter in the lemon filling

☛ Used light butter in the pie crust

Nutrition Scorecard
(per serving)

	Before	After
Calories	402	273
Fat (grams)	17	6
% calories from fat	38	18
Cholesterol (mg)	145	65

1 baked pastry crust (page 59)

Filling

1¼ cups sugar

⅓ cup plus 2 tablespoons cornstarch

⅛ teaspoon salt

1½ cups water

½ cup fresh lemon juice

2 egg yolks, lightly beaten

1 tablespoon finely grated lemon zest

Meringue Topping

4 egg whites

½ teaspoon cream of tartar

½ cup sugar

2 teaspoons finely grated lemon zest

Preheat the oven to 350° F.

To make the filling: In a medium saucepan, combine the 1¼ cups sugar, cornstarch, and salt. Gradually stir in the water and lemon juice. Cook and stir over medium-high heat until thickened and bubbly. Cook and stir 2 minutes more. Remove from the heat. In a small bowl, gradually stir ½ cup of the hot filling by the teaspoonful into the beaten egg yolks, stirring constantly until blended. Pour the egg yolk mixture back into the saucepan, stirring until combined with remaining filling. Bring to a gentle boil over medium heat, stirring constantly. Cook and stir 2 minutes more. Remove from the heat and stir in the 1 tablespoon lemon zest. Pour into *baked* pie shell.

To make the meringue: In a large bowl, beat the egg whites with an electric mixer until foamy. Add the cream of tartar and beat until soft peaks form (tips curl). Gradually beat in the ½ cup sugar, 1 tablespoon at a time. Add the 2 teaspoons lemon zest and beat well until the meringue forms stiff, shiny peaks.

Place about half the meringue around the edge of the warm filling. Use a rubber spatula to carefully seal it to the pie crust. Pile the remaining meringue in the center, then spread to make decorative swirls. Bake for 15 minutes, or until the meringue is golden brown. Let cool on a wire rack.

Poke a Yolk

Many traditional puddings use egg yolks for a thickening agent. Cornstarch can do that job—it can be used for all or part of the yolks. (I generally use 1 tablespoon of cornstarch for each yolk.) You save 5 grams of fat and 215 milligrams of cholesterol for each yolk omitted. Plus you have the added bonus of a recipe that is much easier to make.

Fat-Free Apple Turnovers

Serves 6

❧❧❧❧❧

All the flavor of apple pie packed into individual treats without the fat!

How fat and calories were lowered:

☛ Eliminated butter in the filling

☛ Substituted cornstarch for the flour

☛ Reduced the sugar content

☛ Used a phyllo crust rather than a traditional pastry

Nutrition Scorecard *(per serving)*		
	Before	After
Calories	273	150
Fat (grams)	12	0
% calories from fat	40	0
Cholesterol (mg)	5	0

Filling

1 teaspoon cornstarch

⅓ cup plus 1 tablespoon water

2 cups peeled, chopped apple

⅓ cup packed light brown sugar

¼ teaspoon cinnamon

⅛ teaspoon ground nutmeg

6 phyllo dough sheets

Glaze

¼ cup powdered sugar

1½ teaspoons nonfat milk

¼ teaspoon vanilla extract

Preheat the oven to 375° F. Lightly coat a baking sheet with nonstick vegetable-oil spray and set aside.

To make the filling: In a measuring cup, dissolve the cornstarch in the 1 tablespoon water; set aside.

In a medium saucepan, combine the apples and the ⅓ cup water. Cook and stir on high heat until mixture comes to a boil. Reduce heat to low. Simmer 5 minutes. Stir in the brown sugar, cinnamon, and nutmeg. Simmer 5 minutes, stirring frequently. Stir cornstarch paste into apple mixture. Bring to a boil and boil for 1 minute.

To assemble the turnovers: Place one sheet of the phyllo dough on a large piece of wax paper. Spray the phyllo sheet with nonstick spray. Fold it lengthwise. Spray the folded sheet with nonstick spray. (Keep the remaining phyllo sheets covered with a damp cloth to prevent drying out.) Spoon a mound of about ¼ cup of the apple mixture 1 inch from one end of the folded phyllo strip. Fold the end over the apple mixture at a 45° angle.

Continue folding to form a triangle that encloses the apple mixture (this procedure is like folding a flag). Place the turnover on the prepared baking sheet and repeat the procedure with the remaining phyllo dough to make a total of 6 turnovers. Bake 7 to 10 minutes, or until golden. Let cool on a wire rack.

To make the glaze: In a small bowl, combine the powdered sugar, milk, and vanilla. Stir well. Drizzle over the cooled turnovers. Serve warm or cool.

Sweet Potato Pie

Serves 8

❧❧❧❧❧

What a delicious way to enjoy vitamin A! One serving of this pie provides 100 percent of the adult recommended dietary allowance of this nutrient. Tip: You can use a 40-ounce can of cooked sweet potatoes. When they are drained and mashed, they yield about 2 cups.

How fat and calories were lowered:

- Reduced the amount of brown sugar
- Used evaporated skim milk instead of cream
- Omitted butter from the filling
- Used a lower-fat pie crust

Nutrition Scorecard
(per serving)

	Before	After
Calories	380	292
Fat (grams)	19	5
% calories from fat	43	14
Cholesterol (mg)	82	13

1 unbaked pastry crust (page 59)

Filling

4 egg whites

⅔ cup packed light brown sugar

2 cups mashed, cooked sweet potatoes

1 tablespoon all-purpose flour

1½ teaspoons cinnamon

½ teaspoon ground ginger

½ teaspoon ground nutmeg

¼ teaspoon ground allspice

¼ teaspoon ground cloves

⅛ teaspoon salt

1 (12-ounce) can evaporated skim milk

½ teaspoon imitation rum extract

Preheat the oven to 425° F.

In a medium bowl, beat together the egg whites and brown sugar until light. Beat in the sweet potatoes, flour, cinnamon, ginger, nutmeg, allspice, cloves, salt, evaporated skim milk, and rum extract. Blend thoroughly. Pour the mixture into the unbaked pie shell.

Bake for 15 minutes, then reduce the oven temperature to 325° F. and continue baking 35 to 40 minutes, or until the filling is firm and a knife inserted 1 inch from the edge comes out almost clean. (A little sweet potato will adhere to the knife.)

Let cool on a wire rack. Serve at room temperature or chilled. Cover and refrigerate any leftover pie.

Pear Apple Pie

Serves 8

✄ ✄ ✄ ✄ ✄

The filling is cooked on the stovetop rather than in the oven, because the delicate phyllo burns easily when left in the oven for a long time.

How fat and calories were lowered:

☛ Used fat-free pastry crust

☛ Omitted the butter from filling

☛ Replaced the flour with cornstarch in filling

Nutrition Scorecard
(per serving)

	Before	After
Calories	465	201
Fat (grams)	19	<1
% calories from fat	36	2
Cholesterol (mg)	8	0

Filling

4 large pears, peeled, cored, and thinly
    sliced (about 4 cups)

4 medium apples, peeled, cored, and thinly
    sliced (about 4 cups)

½ cup packed light brown sugar

2 tablespoons fresh lemon juice

¼ cup sugar

2 tablespoons cornstarch

1 teaspoon cinnamon

¼ teaspoon ground nutmeg

1 unbaked Fat-Free Phyllo Crust
    (page 70)

1 sheet phyllo

Preheat the oven to 350° F.

To make the filling: In a 4-quart saucepan, combine pears, apples, brown sugar, and lemon juice. Cook and stir over medium heat until the mixture comes to a boil. Reduce the heat to low and simmer 10 minutes, stirring occasionally, until fruit is soft. Combine white sugar, cornstarch, cinnamon, and nutmeg; add to fruit mixture. Bring to a boil, stirring frequently, and boil for 1 minute. Transfer to prepared phyllo crust.

Cut phyllo sheet in half. Lightly coat each half sheet with nonstick vegetable-oil spray; stack the 2 layers. Fold lengthwise. Cut into 6 strips. Arrange strips over pie filling like a tic-tac-toe arrangement, with 3 horizontal and 3 vertical strips.

Bake for 10 to 15 minutes, or until phyllo is golden. Serve immediately.

Fat-Free Phyllo Crust

Serves 8

✕✕ ✕✕ ✕✕

I often get requests for a fat-free pie crust. This simple but elegant phyllo dough crust does the trick. The key to working with this paper-thin dough is to keep it covered with a damp cloth (but not too damp) to prevent it from drying out and cracking.

How fat and calories were lowered:

🖙 Used a combination of phyllo and nonstick vegetable spray instead of the traditional shortening-and-flour pastry crust.

Nutrition Scorecard
(per serving)

	Before	After
Calories	199	38
Fat (grams)	12	0
% calories from fat	53	0
Cholesterol (mg)	31	0

1 tablespoon sugar	¼ teaspoon cinnamon
1 teaspoon all-purpose flour	4 sheets phyllo

Lightly coat a 9-inch pie pan with nonstick vegetable-oil spray.

In a small bowl or custard cup, combine the sugar, flour, and cinnamon; set aside.

Stack the phyllo sheets and cut them in half crosswise. Cover the sheets with a slightly damp cloth until you are ready to use them. Take one sheet and layer it on the pie pan. Coat it lightly with nonstick vegetable-oil spray and sprinkle about ½ teaspoon of the sugar mixture over it. Repeat with remaining 7 half sheets, layering clockwise at 1-inch intervals until entire pie pan rim is covered. Trim the excess phyllo with kitchen shears. Bake as directed by recipe.

Fudgy Blackbottom Pie

Serves 8

※ ※ ※ ※ ※

Ihis pie is a knockout. The dense chocolate layer will appease the strongest chocolate cravings. I like to use powdered egg whites anytime a recipe calls for eggs to be used uncooked. They greatly reduce the risk of salmonella, because they are pasteurized.

How fat and calories were lowered:

- Eliminated egg yolks and added more cornstarch for thickening
- Used a low-fat chocolate pie crust
- Replaced cream with evaporated skim milk
- Reduced the amount of chocolate chips and added cocoa powder

Nutrition Scorecard
(per serving)

	Before	After
Calories	549	334
Fat (grams)	34	7
% calories from fat	54	19
Cholesterol (mg)	156	3

1 prepared Chocolate Cookie Crust (page 60)

2 tablespoons plus 2 cups evaporated skim milk

1 envelope (2 teaspoons) unflavored gelatin

1¼ cups sugar (divided)

2 tablespoons cornstarch

1 teaspoon vanilla extract

¼ cup unsweetened cocoa powder

½ cup semisweet chocolate, finely chopped (or chocolate chips)

½ teaspoon imitation rum extract

3 tablespoons powdered egg whites (page 44)

½ cup warm water

To make the filling: Put the 2 tablespoons evaporated skim milk in a small bowl and sprinkle the gelatin over it. Stir and set aside to soften.

In a small saucepan, combine ½ cup of the sugar and the cornstarch. Stir in the 2 cups evaporated skim milk. Cook and stir until bubbly, then cook and stir 2 minutes more. Remove from the heat and stir in the vanilla. Divide the mixture in half.

Combine the cocoa powder and ¼ cup of the sugar; stir into one portion of the hot milk mixture until blended. Add chopped chocolate and stir until melted and smooth. Pour into pie shell. Chill.

Stir the softened gelatin mixture into the remaining hot milk mixture until the gelatin dissolves. Stir in the rum extract. Chill to the consistency of corn syrup, stirring occasionally. Remove from the refrigerator (gelatin will continue to set).

In a large bowl, add the powdered egg whites to the warm water. Stir gently until dissolved, about 3 minutes. With an electric mixer on high setting, beat the egg whites until soft peaks form. Gradually add the remaining ½ cup sugar, beating until stiff peaks form. Gently fold into the gelatin mixture. Spread over chocolate layer. Chill for 3 to 4 hours, or until firm.

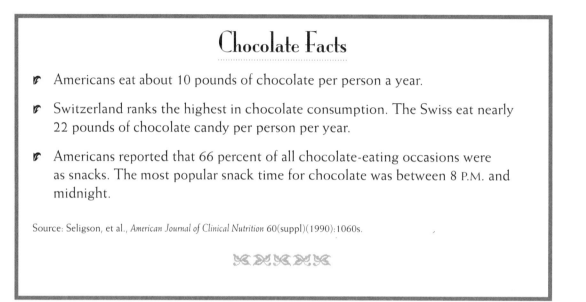

Chocolate Facts

- Americans eat about 10 pounds of chocolate per person a year.

- Switzerland ranks the highest in chocolate consumption. The Swiss eat nearly 22 pounds of chocolate candy per person per year.

- Americans reported that 66 percent of all chocolate-eating occasions were as snacks. The most popular snack time for chocolate was between 8 P.M. and midnight.

Source: Seligson, et al., *American Journal of Clinical Nutrition* 60(suppl)(1990):1060s.

Blueberry Pie (Fat Free, Too)

Serves 8

❈❈❈❈❈

This pie is chock full of blueberries and so delicious. It can also be made with a more traditional pastry crust (page 59).

☛ Replaced pie crust with a fat-free version

☛ Eliminated butter

Nutrition Scorecard
(per serving)

	Before	After
Calories	416	189
Fat (grams)	15	0
% calories from fat	33	2
Cholesterol (mg)	4	0

6 cups fresh blueberries

¾ cup sugar

3 tablespoons cornstarch

1 teaspoon cinnamon

¼ teaspoon ground nutmeg

1 tablespoon fresh lemon juice

1 prepared phyllo crust (page 70)

1 sheet phyllo

Preheat the oven to 350° F.

Rinse and sort the blueberries and pick out and discard any stems. Drain thoroughly on paper towels and pat dry.

In a 4-quart saucepan, combine the sugar, cornstarch, cinnamon, and nutmeg; mix well. Add the blueberries and sprinkle with the lemon juice. Toss lightly to combine. Cook and gently stir over medium heat until the mixture comes to a boil. Cook and stir 2 additional minutes. Remove from the heat and transfer to the prepared phyllo crust.

Cut the phyllo sheet in half crosswise. Lightly coat each half sheet with nonstick vegetable-oil spray. Stack the 2 layers and fold lengthwise. Cut into 6 strips. Arrange the strips over the pie filling like a tic-tac-toe arrangement, with 3 horizontal and 3 vertical strips.

Bake for 20 to 25 minutes, or until the phyllo is golden. Let cool on wire rack. Serve at room temperature.

Puddings

and

Mousses

Chocolate Bread Pudding

Serves 6

✂ ✂ ✂ ✂ ✂

This bread pudding has an extra-healthy twist—whole-wheat bread is used instead of traditional white bread. Nobody will know the difference. For a smooth texture, use a fine-textured whole-wheat bread rather than a type that contains cracked wheat, wheat berries, or extra bran.

How fat and calories were lowered:

☛ Reduced the amount of chocolate chips and replaced them in part with baking cocoa

☛ Used evaporated skim milk instead of whole milk and cream

☛ Used egg whites instead of whole eggs

☛ Eliminated butter

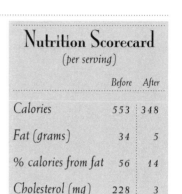

Nutrition Scorecard
(per serving)

	Before	After
Calories	553	348
Fat (grams)	34	5
% calories from fat	56	14
Cholesterol (mg)	228	3

2 cups evaporated skim milk	6 slices whole-wheat bread
⅓ cup semisweet chocolate chips	¼ cup coffee liqueur
¼ cup unsweetened cocoa powder	7 egg whites, slightly beaten
¾ cup sugar	

Lightly coat a 10-cup soufflé dish or casserole with nonstick vegetable-oil spray.

In microwavable bowl, scald 1 cup of the evaporated skim milk in the microwave (about 60 seconds on High). Stir in chocolate chips and stir until melted. Combine cocoa powder and sugar; add to melted chocolate chip mixture. Stir until dissolved; set aside.

Trim the crusts off the bread and cut the bread into ½-inch cubes; transfer to the prepared dish. Combine the remaining 1 cup evaporated milk, the coffee liqueur, and the egg whites. Add the egg white mixture to the chocolate mixture and mix well with a whisk. Pour over the bread cube mixture and stir to combine. Cover and refrigerate overnight.

Preheat oven to 325° F. Bake pudding for about 1 hour, until puffed and golden and center is almost set. Serve warm.

Chocolate Tapioca

Serves 6

❧❧❧❧❧

I've always enjoyed lumpy food, especially tapioca pudding. The little clumps of tapioca embedded in chocolate extend the pudding pleasure.

How fat and calories were lowered:

☛ Replaced part of the chocolate chips with cocoa powder

☛ Used nonfat milk instead of whole milk

☛ Reduced the amount of sugar

☛ Eliminated the egg

Nutrition Scorecard
(per serving)

	Before	After
Calories	220	190
Fat (grams)	8	3
% calories from fat	31	12
Cholesterol (mg)	51	3

⅔ cup sugar

⅓ cup quick tapioca

¼ cup unsweetened cocoa powder

2¾ cups nonfat milk

3 tablespoons semisweet chocolate chips

1 teaspoon vanilla extract

In a medium saucepan, mix together the sugar, tapioca, and cocoa powder. Add the nonfat milk. Over medium heat, cook and stir until mixture comes to a boil. Continue boiling for 1 additional minute, stirring continuously. Remove from the heat. Stir in the chocolate chips until blended and melted. Stir in the vanilla. Transfer to 6 custard cups. Cover and chill.

Quick Tip

Can't wait for that pudding to cool? Immerse the pan in ice water and let it sit for about 15 minutes, then transfer the pudding to dessert dishes. It will cool much faster because heat transfers more quickly in water than in air.

❧❧❧❧❧

Chocolate Fudge Pudding

Serves 6

✂✂✂✂✂

This pudding will send you straight to chocolate heaven with its rich flavor.

How fat and calories were lowered:

☛ Used cocoa powder instead of baking chocolate

☛ Used nonfat milk instead of whole milk

☛ Eliminated the butter

☛ Replaced the egg yolks with additional cornstarch

Nutrition Scorecard *(per serving)*		
	Before	After
Calories	255	164
Fat (grams)	15	4
% calories from fat	48	22
Cholesterol (mg)	87	1

½ cup sugar

⅓ cup unsweetened cocoa powder

3 tablespoons cornstarch

2 cups nonfat milk

⅓ cup chocolate chips

1 teaspoon vanilla extract

In a medium saucepan, combine the sugar, cocoa powder, and cornstarch. Add the nonfat milk. Cook and stir over medium heat until the mixture thickens and comes to a boil. Continue stirring and boil for 1 additional minute. Remove from the heat. Stir in the chocolate chips, mixing until melted. Stir in the vanilla. Pour into 6 dessert dishes and cover the surface of the puddings with plastic wrap to prevent a skin from forming. Chill.

Carob vs. Chocolate

Some people will use carob instead of chocolate because it's perceived as being more healthful. But when carob is made into candy such as carob chips, it has just as much fat as chocolate chips. Unfortunately, the fat used in carob is often hydrogenated palm oil, an artery-clogging saturated fat. One benefit of carob is that it has no caffeinelike compounds.

✂✂✂✂✂

Vanilla Bean Pudding

Serves 6

✠ ✠ ✠ ✠ ✠

Such rich flavor! *(Shhh—don't tell them there's no fat.)*
How fat and calories were lowered:

✒ Reduced the amount of sugar

✒ Replaced milk with a combination of evaporated skim milk and fresh nonfat milk

✒ Eliminated egg yolks and butter

Nutrition Scorecard		
(per serving)		
	Before	After
Calories	240	165
Fat (grams)	9	0
% calories from fat	35	1
Cholesterol (mg)	164	3

⅔ cup sugar

¼ cup cornstarch

1 (12-ounce) can evaporated skim milk

1½ cups nonfat milk

2½-inch piece vanilla bean, split lengthwise

In a medium saucepan, combine the sugar and cornstarch. Stir in the evaporated skim milk and fresh nonfat milk. Using the tip of a knife, scrape the seeds from the vanilla bean into the milk mixture; add the vanilla bean pod. Cook and stir over medium heat until the mixture is thickened and bubbly. Cook and stir one minute more. Remove from heat. Carefully remove and discard vanilla bean pod. Pour into 6 dessert dishes. Cover with plastic wrap. Chill.

Canned Milk—Double the Calcium

Evaporated skim milk has twice the calcium, ounce for ounce, than regular skim or whole milk—and offers rich texture and nutritional advantage in puddings.

✠ ✠ ✠ ✠ ✠

Easy Chocolate Mousse

Serves 6

✕✕ ✕✕ ✕✕

Mousse is often described as a light dessert in reference to its feathery texture, but the traditional version is loaded with fat. It's hard to believe that even a moderate portion has 29 grams of fat.

How I cut the calories and whittled the fat to only 5 grams per serving:

☞ Used fat-free cream cheese instead of the full-fat version

☞ Replaced heavy cream with a combination of light nondairy whipped topping and marshmallow creme

☞ Reduced the amount of sugar

Nutrition Scorecard
(per serving)

	Before	After
Calories	374	265
Fat (grams)	29	5
% calories from fat	66	16
Cholesterol (mg)	96	7

8 ounces fat-free cream cheese

⅔ cup sugar

3 tablespoons unsweetened cocoa powder

¼ cup semisweet chocolate chips

1 cup marshmallow creme

½ (8-ounce) tub thawed frozen light nondairy whipped topping

In a medium bowl, beat together the fat-free cream cheese, sugar, and cocoa powder with an electric mixer at medium speed until smooth; set aside.

In a large microwavable bowl, melt the chocolate chips in the microwave on High, stirring every 30 seconds until smooth. Add the marshmallow creme and stir with a wooden spoon until blended. Gradually stir in the cream cheese mixture. Fold in the nondairy whipped topping. Turn the mousse into 6 dessert dishes. Cover and chill at least one hour.

Easy Mocha Mousse

Prepare as directed above, but dissolve 1 teaspoon instant coffee granules into 1 teaspoon of milk and beat this in with the cream cheese mixture.

Hazelnut Mousse

Serves 6

❧❧❧❧❧

The flecks of toasted hazelnuts add a wonderful texture and flavor. You can substitute brandy for the hazelnut liqueur.

How fat and calories were lowered:

☞ Reduced the amount of hazelnuts

☞ Used a combination of nondairy whipped topping, fat-free cream cheese, and marshmallow creme instead of whipping cream

☞ Eliminated the eggs

Nutrition Scorecard
(per serving)

	Before	After
Calories	482	295
Fat (grams)	34	5
% calories from fat	62	17
Cholesterol (mg)	200	7

¼ cup chopped hazelnuts, toasted

1 cup powdered sugar

8 ounces fat-free cream cheese

¾ cup marshmallow creme

2 tablespoons Frangelico (hazelnut liqueur)

1½ cups thawed frozen light nondairy whipped topping

Grind the hazelnuts with 1 tablespoon of the powdered sugar in a food processor until the mixture resembles fine bread crumbs. In a large mixing bowl, beat together ground hazelnuts, the remaining sugar, the fat-free cream cheese, and the marshmallow creme with an electric mixer until smooth. Stir in the Frangelico. Fold in the whipped topping. Spoon mousse into goblets. Cover and chill at least 1 hour.

Crème Brûlée

Serves 5

❈ ❈ ❈ ❈ ❈

This dessert still remains rich and creamy with only a fraction of the fat. Rather than baking the custard, I used a classic stovetop method to maintain the creamy texture without all the fat.

How fat and calories were lowered:

☞ Reduced the amount of egg yolks and replaced them in part with cornstarch

☞ Greatly reduced the whipping cream and replaced it with a combination of evaporated skim milk and fresh nonfat milk

Nutrition Scorecard *(per serving)*		
	Before	After
Calories	363	189
Fat (grams)	29	7
% calories from fat	71	31

⅓ cup sugar

2 tablespoons cornstarch

1 cup evaporated skim milk

¼ cup heavy cream

¼ cup fresh nonfat milk

4-inch vanilla bean, split

2 egg yolks, slightly beaten

2 tablespoons packed light brown sugar

In the top part of a double boiler, combine the white sugar and cornstarch. Gradually stir in the evaporated skim milk, heavy cream, and nonfat milk. Scrape the seeds from the vanilla bean and add both the seeds and the pod to the milk mixture. Place the double boiler over (not in) simmering water. Using a whisk, stir the mixture constantly 10 minutes until thickened. Remove the vanilla bean. Gradually stir a few teaspoons of the custard mixture into the beaten yolks, mixing constantly until blended. When you have added about ½ cup, pour the yolk mixture back into the pan, stirring constantly until combined.

Place the pan over the simmering water again. Cook for 5 to 7 minutes, until the mixture is thick and smooth. Remove from the heat. Transfer to five ½-cup ramekins or five ⅔-cup custard cups. Let cool to room temperature. Cover each ramekin with plastic wrap and refrigerate until very cold, at least 3 hours, or it can be covered and chilled overnight. (The mixture needs to be covered to prevent a skin forming on the surface.)

Shortly before serving, preheat the broiler with the rack about 3 inches from the heat. Place the custards in a baking pan and surround with ice. Sieve a thin, even layer of the brown sugar over the custards. Place under the broiler just until the sugar melts (about 1 to 3 minutes). Watch carefully to prevent burning. Serve immediately.

White Chocolate Mousse with Raspberry Compote

Serves 8

❈ ❈ ❈ ❈

I *always get "oohs and aahhs" with this dessert. I love to serve it at dinner parties, because you can make it the day before and it's ready to serve straight out of the fridge. I am told by my epicurean friends that one should remove the seeds from raspberry sauces, but I prefer the texture and extra fiber, especially in this almost too-elegant dessert. If you wish, you can remove the seeds by pushing the raspberry sauce through a sieve.*

How fat and calories were lowered:

🐦 Reduced the amount of white chocolate

🐦 Reduced the amount of sugar

🐦 Replaced whipping cream with a combination of fat-free cream cheese and light nondairy whipped topping

Nutrition Scorecard
(per serving)

	Before	After
Calories	544	295
Fat (grams)	38	5
% calories from fat	62	16
Cholesterol (mg)	93	7

Raspberry Compote

1 (12-ounce) bag frozen raspberries

⅓ cup sugar

1 teaspoon cornstarch

White Chocolate Mousse

3 ounces good-quality white chocolate, chopped

1 cup marshmallow creme

8 ounces fat-free cream cheese, at room temperature

1 teaspoon fresh lemon juice

4 ounces (1½ cups) thawed frozen light nondairy whipped topping

To make the raspberry compote: Combine the frozen raspberries and sugar in a medium saucepan. Bring to a boil over medium-high heat, stirring constantly. Set aside about 1 tablespoon of the raspberry liquid. Boil the raspberry mixture, stirring occasionally, until the volume is reduced by half, about 8 minutes. Combine the reserved raspberry juice and the cornstarch and mix until smooth; add to raspberry mixture. Cook and stir until thickened, about 1 minute. Remove from the heat and let cool.

To make the mousse: In a microwavable bowl, melt the white chocolate in a microwave, on High setting, stirring every 30 seconds, until smooth (about 2 minutes). Add the marshmallow creme and stir with wooden spoon until blended.

In a large bowl, beat the cream cheese with an electric mixer on medium speed until creamy. Add the white chocolate mixture and beat until smooth. Stir in the lemon juice. Using a rubber spatula, fold in the nondairy whipped topping.

To assemble: Turn half of the mousse out into 8 wineglasses. Layer half of the raspberry compote over the mousse layer. Repeat the layering with the remaining mousse and compote. Cover and chill at least 1 hour. (It tastes even better if you allow it to chill overnight.)

Sweet Tooth and Obesity

Obese individuals are no different from normal weight individuals in preferences for sweet foods.

Source: Anderson, G., *American Journal of Clinical Nutrition* 62(suppl)(1995):199s.

✂ ✂ ✂ ✂ ✂

Sweet Potato Pudding

Serves 8

❈ ❈ ❈ ❈

Accented by orange zest and crowned with a light orange glaze, this pudding is great when just made and terrific as a leftover for breakfast! A small amount of light butter makes a substantial difference to the flavor for the glaze (and there's only 1 gram of fat per serving). I tried making the glaze without any butter, and it just wasn't quite as good.

How fat and calories were lowered:

☛ Eliminated the butter from the pudding and greatly reduced the amount in the glaze

☛ Used egg whites instead of whole eggs

☛ Reduced the amount of sugar

☛ Eliminated the alcohol from the glaze (it originally had rum)

Nutrition Scorecard
(per serving)

	Before	After
Calories	355	204
Fat (grams)	14	1
% calories from fat	37	4
Cholesterol (mg)	138	2

Pudding

1 (29-ounce) can sweet potatoes, drained, or 3 cups cooked and cubed

4 egg whites

⅓ cup packed light brown sugar

2 tablespoons all-purpose flour

1 teaspoon finely grated orange zest (reserve orange)

½ teaspoon ground nutmeg

Glaze

¼ cup fresh orange juice

½ cup packed light brown sugar

1 tablespoon light butter

Preheat the oven to 350° F. Lightly coat 8 ramekins or custard cups with nonstick vegetable-oil spray.

To make the pudding: Using a food processor or electric mixer, process or mix the sweet potato, egg whites, the ⅓ cup brown sugar, flour, orange zest, and nutmeg until smooth. Transfer the mixture to the prepared ramekins.

To make the glaze: Squeeze the juice from the reserved orange into a liquid measuring cup. Add additional fresh orange juice to total ¼ cup. In a small saucepan, combine the ½ cup brown sugar, orange juice, and light butter. Cook and stir over medium-high heat until boiling. Drizzle the glaze over the surface of the sweet potato mixture.

Bake about 30 minutes, until the pudding is set and the glaze is bubbly. Let cool to luke-warm on a wire rack before serving.

Dessert Behavior: Men vs. Women

Women are more likely than men to eat dessert if someone else orders it first.

Source: Guarino, et al., *Psychological Reports* 75(1994):603.

Healthy Homestyle Desserts

Fat-Free Apricot Fool

Serves 6

✂ ✂ ✂ ✂ ✂

If you love apricots, you'll love the intense fruit flavor of this dessert. How fat and calories were lowered:

✐ Used nonfat vanilla yogurt instead of heavy cream

✐ Reduced the amount of sugar

✐ Eliminated the sliced almonds

Nutrition Scorecard
(per serving)

	Before	After
Calories	386	222
Fat (grams)	21	0
% calories from fat	50	0
Cholesterol (mg)	68	0

½ pound (about 1½ cups) dried apricots

2⅓ cups cold water

¾ cup sugar

1 (¼-ounce) envelope unflavored gelatin

¼ cup amaretto (almond liqueur)

¼ teaspoon almond extract

2 cups nonfat vanilla yogurt

Combine the apricots, water, and sugar in a heavy saucepan and bring to a boil over medium-high heat, stirring occasionally. Cover, reduce the heat to low, and simmer until the apricots are tender, about 10 minutes. Add the gelatin and stir until dissolved. Remove from the heat. Set aside to cool slightly.

Puree the apricots and syrup in two batches in a food processor or blender. Stir in the amaretto and almond extract. Cover and refrigerate until slightly chilled but not cold.

Stir the apricot puree once or twice to loosen it. Gently fold in the vanilla yogurt until blended. Transfer to 6 goblets. Cover and refrigerate for at least 2 hours.

Orange Essence Prune Whip

Serves 6

✂ ✂ ✂ ✂ ✂

Prunes have a wonderful flavor and a rich texture, which is why they're so versatile in many desserts. This dessert could easily double as breakfast.

How fat and calories were lowered:

☛ Used nonfat yogurt instead of cream

Nutrition Scorecard *(per serving)*	Before	After
Calories	243	148
Fat (grams)	15	0
% calories from fat	52	0
Cholesterol (mg)	54	0

1½ cups pitted prunes

1½ cups water

1 teaspoon finely grated orange zest

½ teaspoon finely grated lemon zest

½ teaspoon cinnamon

2 cups nonfat vanilla yogurt

Combine the prunes and water in a heavy saucepan; bring to a boil over medium-high heat, stirring occasionally. Cover, reduce the heat to low, and simmer until the prunes are tender, about 7 minutes. Remove from the heat. Set aside to cool slightly.

Puree the prunes and their cooking liquid in two batches in a food processor or blender. Stir in the orange zest, lemon zest, and cinnamon. Cover and refrigerate until slightly chilled but not cold.

Stir the prune puree once or twice to loosen it. Gently fold in the vanilla yogurt until blended. Transfer to 6 goblets. Cover and refrigerate at least 2 hours.

Prunes May Lower Cholesterol

Prunes are rich in soluble fiber, primarily from pectin. The high pectin content may play a role in reducing blood cholesterol.

Source: *American Journal of Clinical Nutrition* 53(1991):1259.

✂ ✂ ✂ ✂ ✂

Orange Cream Cheese Bavarian

Serves 6

❊ ❊ ❊ ❊

*T*his is also a healthy dessert snack for kids—just pour it into little custard cups instead of a gelatin mold.

How fat and calories were lowered:

☞ Used nonfat vanilla yogurt instead of heavy cream

☞ Replaced regular cream cheese with fat-free cream cheese

☞ Dissolved gelatin in milk rather than water for added body

Nutrition Scorecard *(per serving)*		
	Before	After
Calories	321	101
Fat *(grams)*	28	0
% calories from fat	77	0
Cholesterol *(mg)*	96	7

¼ cup nonfat milk

1 (¼-ounce) envelope unflavored gelatin

1 cup nonfat vanilla yogurt

⅔ cup thawed orange juice concentrate

1 tablespoon fresh lemon juice

½ teaspoon finely grated orange zest

8 ounces fat-free cream cheese, at room temperature

¼ cup sugar

Lightly coat a 4-cup mold or bowl with nonstick vegetable-oil spray and set aside.

In a small saucepan, combine the nonfat milk and gelatin. Cook over medium-low heat, stirring constantly, until the gelatin is dissolved and the mixture coats the back of a spoon (do not boil). Remove saucepan from heat.

In a small bowl, combine the yogurt, orange juice concentrate, lemon juice, and orange zest. Stir in the gelatin mixture.

In a large bowl, beat together the fat-free cream cheese and sugar with an electric mixer until smooth. Fold in the orange juice mixture. Pour the mixture into the prepared mold and refrigerate until set, 3 to 4 hours.

Quick

Breads

and

Muffins

Maple-Frosted "Doughnuts"

Serves 6

❧ ❧ ❧ ❧ ❧

I don't usually dream about food, but one night I had a vivid dream about low-fat maple doughnuts. They were airy, with a light springiness upon biting into them—similar to a cruller. That dream inspired these doughnuts. Up until then, every low-fat doughnut I tried resembled a muffin with frosting. I used a popover baking technique for a lovely texture. Using a mini Bundt muffin pan is critical to the texture and appearance.

How fat and calories were lowered:

☛ Eliminated frying

☛ Used egg whites instead of whole eggs

☛ Replaced the whole milk with nonfat milk

☛ Eliminated the butter in the batter

Nutrition Scorecard
(per serving)

	Before	After
Calories	210	122
Fat (grams)	12	1
% calories from fat	50	7
Cholesterol (mg)	20	0

Dough

2 egg whites

½ cup nonfat milk

1 teaspoon canola oil

¼ cup whole-wheat flour

¼ cup all-purpose flour

¼ cup powdered sugar

⅛ teaspoon ground nutmeg

⅛ teaspoon cinnamon

Maple Frosting

½ cup confectioners' sugar

2 tablespoons pure maple syrup

1 teaspoon maple extract

¾ teaspoon nonfat milk

Preheat the oven to 400° F. Lightly coat a mini Bundt muffin pan (six muffin cups) with nonstick vegetable-oil spray.

To make the dough: In a medium bowl, combine the egg whites, nonfat milk, and oil. Add the whole-wheat and all-purpose flours, the powdered sugar, nutmeg, and cinnamon. Beat with a wire whisk until smooth.

Divide the batter equally among the six prepared muffin cups. Bake for 20 minutes. Turn the heat off and leave the doughnuts in the oven for 5 minutes. Remove the doughnuts from the oven. Remove the doughnuts from the pan and let cool on a wire rack. Frost when cool.

To make the maple frosting: In a small bowl, combine the powdered sugar, maple syrup, maple extract, and nonfat milk. Mix until smooth. Ice the doughnuts by dipping the tops in the frosting. After the frosting is set on the doughnuts, drizzle the remaining frosting equally among the doughnuts.

Quality Oils

When a recipe calls for vegetable oil, I prefer using canola oil, because it is the lowest in saturated fat. (Saturated fat is the chief dietary culprit that raises cholesterol in the blood.) Here are the saturated fat contents of cooking oils and shortening:

% Saturated Fat Content	
6	Canola oil
10	Safflower oil
11	Sunflower oil
13	Corn oil
14	Olive oil
28	Vegetable shortening
40	Lard

❈ ❈ ❈ ❈ ❈

Giant Carrot–Apple Muffins

Makes 6

⌘ ⌘ ⌘ ⌘

These bakery-size muffins are absolutely delicious. You can make these smaller by using a standard 12-cup pan, but hands down everyone prefers the mega-size. They are healthy enough, however, to call them "breakfast."

How fat and calories were lowered:

☞ Reduced the amount of the sugar, walnuts, and coconut

☞ Replaced the oil with a combination of applesauce and buttermilk

Nutrition Scorecard
(per serving)

	Before	After
Calories	737	398
Fat (grams)	39	5
% calories from fat	47	15
Cholesterol (mg)	53	0

1 cup whole-wheat flour

1 cup all-purpose flour

¾ cup sugar

2 teaspoons baking powder

2 teaspoons cinnamon

½ teaspoon baking soda

2 cups finely shredded carrots

1 medium apple, peeled and shredded

½ cup raisins

¼ cup chopped walnuts

¼ cup flaked coconut

6 egg whites, lightly beaten

½ cup buttermilk

⅓ cup unsweetened applesauce

2 teaspoons vanilla extract

Preheat the oven to 350° F. Coat 6 large, 3-inch muffin cups with nonstick vegetable-oil spray.

In a large bowl, stir together the whole-wheat flour, all-purpose flour, sugar, baking powder, cinnamon, and baking soda. Stir in the carrots, apple, raisins, walnuts, and coconut.

In a separate bowl, stir together egg whites, buttermilk, applesauce, and vanilla. Add the liquid ingredients all at once to the flour mixture and stir just until moistened. Gently spoon the batter into the prepared muffin cups until each one is nearly full.

Bake about 30 minutes, or until a toothpick inserted near the center comes out clean. Let the muffins cool in the pan for 5 minutes. Then remove the muffins and let them cool on a wire rack.

Buttermilk Spice "Doughnuts"

Makes 6

※ ※ ※ ※ ※

"This is the best doughnut I've ever had," declared my eight-year-old niece. I like my frostings a little on the thin side. If you want a thicker texture, use less milk.

How fat and calories were lowered:

☛ Eliminated frying

☛ Used egg whites instead of whole eggs

☛ Eliminated butter in the batter

Nutrition Scorecard
(per serving)

	Before	After
Calories	210	115
Fat (grams)	12	1
% calories from fat	50	9
Cholesterol (mg)	20	0

Dough

3 egg whites

½ cup buttermilk

1 teaspoon canola oil

¼ cup whole-wheat flour

¼ cup all-purpose flour

⅓ cup powdered sugar

⅛ teaspoon ground nutmeg

⅛ teaspoon cinnamon

⅛ teaspoon ground cloves

Vanilla Frosting

½ cup powdered sugar

1 tablespoon nonfat milk

½ teaspoon vanilla extract

Preheat the oven to 400° F. Lightly coat a Bundt muffin pan (six muffin cups) with non-stick vegetable-oil spray.

To make the dough: In a medium bowl, combine the egg whites, buttermilk, and oil. Add the whole-wheat and all-purpose flours, powdered sugar, nutmeg, cinnamon, and cloves. Beat until smooth with a wire whisk.

Divide the batter equally among the six prepared muffin cups. Bake for 20 minutes. Remove the doughnuts from the oven. Remove the doughnuts from pan and let them cool on a wire rack. Frost when cool.

To make the vanilla frosting: In a small bowl, combine the powdered sugar, nonfat milk, and vanilla. Mix until smooth. Frost the doughnuts by dipping the tops in the frosting. After the frosting is set on the doughnuts, drizzle the remaining frosting equally among the doughnuts.

Mississippi Mud Muffins

Makes 18 muffins

❈ ❈ ❈ ❈ ❈

Mmmm, mmmm, *just like a mini cheesecake surrounded by a choco-late muffin with bits of chocolate.*

How fat and calories were lowered:

☛ Used fat-free cream cheese instead of regular cream cheese

☛ Replaced whole eggs with egg whites

☛ Used a combination of applesauce and buttermilk in place of the oil

☛ Reduced the amount of chocolate chips and replaced reg-ular-size chips with mini chips

Nutrition Scorecard
(per serving)

	Before	After
Calories	217	130
Fat (grams)	12	2
% calories from fat	48	11
Cholesterol (mg)	37	3

Filling

8 ounces fat-free cream cheese, at room
    temperature

⅓ cup sugar

2 egg whites, lightly beaten

⅓ cup mini chocolate chips

Muffins

1 cup all-purpose flour

1 cup sugar

¼ cup whole-wheat flour

⅓ cup unsweetened cocoa powder

½ teaspoon baking soda

¾ cup buttermilk

⅓ cup unsweetened applesauce

2 egg whites, lightly beaten

1 teaspoon vanilla extract

To make the filling: In a medium bowl, beat together the fat-free cream cheese and the ⅓ cup sugar. Beat in 2 egg whites just until mixed. (Do not overmix, or the fat-free cream cheese will become runny.) Stir in the chips.

To make the muffins: Preheat the oven to 350° F. Lightly coat 18 cupcake cups with vegetable-oil spray.

In a large mixing bowl, combine the all-purpose flour, sugar, whole-wheat flour, cocoa powder, and baking soda.

In a small bowl, beat together the buttermilk, applesauce, egg whites, and vanilla. Add the liquid ingredients all at once to the flour mixture and stir until blended and smooth.

Spoon the batter evenly into prepared muffin cups. Top each with some of the cream cheese filling mixture.

Bake 30 to 35 minutes, or until a toothpick inserted near the center comes out clean. Let the muffins cool, in the pan, on a wire rack for 5 minutes. Then remove the muffins and let them cool on the wire rack.

Americans consume an average of 133 pounds of sugar per person each year (including corn syrup and other sweeteners).

Source: *University of California at Berkeley Wellness Letter*, December 1989, 4.

Blueberry Buckle Bread

Serves 9

❧❧❧❧❧

Tbis snack bread has more blueberries per bite than any blueberry muffin I've ever eaten, and it's very easy to make. The glaze adds a rich, buttery flavor, yet there is only a tiny amount of fat—2 grams—for each generous slice of bread.

How fat and calories were lowered:

☞ Replaced butter with a combination of applesauce and buttermilk

☞ Used egg whites instead of a whole egg

☞ In the glaze, used light butter instead of regular butter

Nutrition Scorecard
(per serving)

	Before	After
Calories	263	201
Fat (grams)	9	2
% calories from fat	30	7
Cholesterol (mg)	46	4

Bread

2 cups fresh or thawed frozen blueberries

1 cup all-purpose flour

¾ cup sugar

½ cup whole-wheat flour

2 teaspoons baking powder

½ teaspoon finely grated lemon zest

⅛ teaspoon salt

2 egg whites

⅓ cup buttermilk

2 tablespoons unsweetened applesauce

1 teaspoon fresh lemon juice

Glaze

2 tablespoons light butter

¼ cup sugar

1 tablespoon fresh lemon juice

Preheat the oven to 350° F. Lightly coat an 8x8x2-inch baking pan with nonstick vegetable-oil spray.

To make the bread: Rinse the fresh blueberries, discarding any stems or blemished berries. If using frozen berries, drain the thawed berries.

In a small bowl, combine the all-purpose flour, the ¾ cup sugar, and the whole-wheat flour, baking powder, lemon zest, and salt.

In a medium bowl, beat the egg whites with an electric mixer until foamy. Add the buttermilk, the applesauce, and the 1 teaspoon lemon juice and mix until blended. Add the flour mixture and mix until blended. Gently fold in the berries by hand.

Spread the batter in the prepared pan. Bake 35 to 40 minutes, or until a toothpick inserted near the center comes out clean. Just before the bread is done, prepare the glaze.

To make the glaze: In a small saucepan, melt the light butter. Stir in the ¼ cup sugar and the 1 tablespoon lemon juice. Cook and stir over low heat until the mixture is bubbly. Remove from the heat.

When the bread tests done, pour the glaze over the top. Return the glazed bread to the oven and broil 3 inches from the heat for 1 to 2 minutes, or until the glaze bubbles. Watch carefully to avoid overbrowning.

Trans Fat: Butter vs. Margarine—Which Is Better?

Margarine isn't as terrific as once thought. Here's why. To make margarine, hydrogen is added to a liquid oil. This turns the oil into a hard or spreadable fat. The problem is that this process creates a new type of fat, trans fatty acids. Trans fatty acids behave like artery-clogging saturated fat. While this at first glance is troubling to margarine users, it's important to keep in mind that over the past forty years there have been several studies comparing butter with margarine. Nearly every time, margarine outperformed butter on lowering cholesterol in the blood. Even when you factor in the trans fatty acids in margarine, it is still three times lower in saturated fat than butter. That said, when it comes to taste, butter wins hands down. My strategy when making desserts is to go as low as tolerable on the fat. When nothing else will do flavorwise, I will use butter in very small amounts.

When you do choose a margarine, opt for the tub version rather than stick. Tub margarines are lower in both trans fatty acids and saturated fat. Better yet, go for the light tub margarines—they are even lower. Do be sure that the first ingredient listed is a liquid oil.

Fats Stats for 1 Tablespoon

	Calories	Fat (grams) (total)	Saturated Fat (grams)	Cholesterol (mg)
Margarine, stick	102	11.4	2.2	0
Margarine, tub	102	11.4	2.0	0
Butter	102	11.5	7.2	31
Butter, light	50	5.5	4.0	15

Source: *American Journal of Clinical Nutrition* 62(1995):657.

Sweet Potato Bread (Fat-Free, Too)

Serves 12

✵✵✵✵✵

This bread is incredibly moist, with almost a steamed-bread texture. Canned pumpkin can be substituted for the sweet potatoes.

How fat and calories were lowered:

- Used a combination of applesauce and buttermilk instead of butter
- Replaced whole eggs with egg whites

Nutrition Scorecard
(per serving)

	Before	After
Calories	224	154
Fat (grams)	9	0
% calories from fat	35	2
Cholesterol (mg)	56	0

1 cup all-purpose flour

1 cup sugar

½ cup whole-wheat flour

1 teaspoon baking powder

½ teaspoon cinnamon

¼ teaspoon ground nutmeg

4 egg whites

2 cups mashed sweet potatoes

⅓ cup buttermilk

2 tablespoons unsweetened applesauce

Preheat the oven to 350° F. Lightly coat an 8x5x3-inch loaf pan with nonstick vegetable-oil spray.

In a small bowl, combine the all-purpose flour, sugar, whole-wheat flour, baking powder, cinnamon, and nutmeg.

In a large bowl, using an electric mixer, beat the egg whites with the sweet potatoes until smooth. Add the buttermilk and applesauce and mix until blended. Add flour mixture and mix until blended. Pour the batter into the prepared pan.

Bake 45 to 50 minutes, or until a toothpick inserted near the center comes out clean. Let cool on a wire rack.

Apple Streusel Muffins

Serves 6

❉❉❉❉❉

The fat-free sour cream adds a terrific flavor and texture. Be sure to use a brand that has no gelatin. The gelatin breaks down at high temperatures.

How fat and calories were lowered:

☞ Used applesauce instead of butter

☞ Replaced whole eggs with egg whites

☞ Used fat-free sour cream instead of regular sour cream

☞ Used light butter instead of regular butter in the topping

Nutrition Scorecard
(per serving)

	Before	After
Calories	548	357
Fat (grams)	22	3
% calories from fat	35	6
Cholesterol (mg)	119	5

Muffins

1 cup whole-wheat flour

1 cup all-purpose flour

¾ cup sugar

1½ teaspoons cinnamon

1 teaspoon baking powder

½ teaspoon baking soda

4 egg whites

1 cup fat-free sour cream (containing no gelatin)

⅓ cup buttermilk

¼ cup unsweetened applesauce

1 cup finely chopped peeled apple

Topping

¼ cup sugar

3 tablespoons all-purpose flour

¼ teaspoon cinnamon

2 tablespoons light butter

To make the muffins: Preheat the oven to 400° F. Lightly coat 6 3-inch muffin cups with nonstick vegetable-oil spray.

In a medium bowl, combine the whole-wheat flour, the 1 cup all-purpose flour, the ¾ cup sugar, the 1½ teaspoons cinnamon, and the baking powder and baking soda.

In a large bowl, beat egg whites with an electric mixer until foamy. Add the sour cream, buttermilk, and applesauce and mix until blended. Add the flour mixture and mix until blended. Gently fold in the chopped apples. Spoon the batter into the prepared muffin cups.

To make the topping: In a small bowl, stir together the ¼ cup sugar, the 3 tablespoons all-purpose flour, and the ¼ teaspoon cinnamon. Using a pastry blender or two knives, cut in the light butter until the mixture resembles coarse crumbs. Sprinkle a portion of the topping (about 1 tablespoon) on each muffin.

Bake the muffins for 20 to 25 minutes, or until the tops are golden.

Sugar Soothes Crying Infants

Infants undergoing circumcision and then given a pacifier dipped in sugar water cried 18 percent less than infants given a plain pacifier.

Source: J. W. White and M. Wolraich, *American Journal of Clinical Nutrition* 62(suppl)(1995):245s.

Dried-Cherry Muffins (Fat-Free, Too)

Makes 6 large muffins

Ɗᴤ Ɗᴤ Ɗᴤ Ɗᴤ Ɗᴤ

These are my husband's favorite muffins.
How fat and calories were lowered:

- Replaced the butter with a combination of applesauce and buttermilk

- Used egg whites instead of a whole egg

Nutrition Scorecard
(per serving)

	Before	After
Calories	420	326
Fat (grams)	13	0
% calories from fat	29	2
Cholesterol (mg)	69	1

1 cup all-purpose flour

¾ cup whole-wheat flour

¾ cup sugar

1 tablespoon baking powder

2 egg whites

⅔ cup buttermilk

⅓ cup unsweetened applesauce

1 teaspoon almond extract

1 cup dried cherries

Preheat the oven to 400° F. Lightly coat a large muffin tin (six 3-inch-wide cups) with nonstick vegetable-oil spray.

In a large bowl, combine the flours, sugar, and baking powder; make a well in the center. In a medium bowl, beat the egg whites until foamy. Add the buttermilk, applesauce, and almond extract; add to dry ingredients. Fold in the dried cherries. Pour the batter into the prepared muffin cups.

Bake 22 to 25 minutes. Let cool 5 minutes, in the pan, on a wire rack. Transfer muffins to the rack to cool completely.

Raspberry Dapple Muffins (Fat-Free, Too)

Makes 6 large muffins

❈ ❈ ❈ ❈ ❈

These are my favorite muffins; in fact, one fellow admirer called this the "muffin of the gods." You can also use blackberries instead of raspberries.

How fat and calories were lowered:

☛ Replaced butter with a combination of applesauce and buttermilk

☛ Used egg whites instead of a whole egg

Nutrition Scorecard (per serving)		
	Before	After
Calories	370	227
Fat (grams)	14	0
% calories from fat	33	3
Cholesterol (mg)	69	0

1 cup all-purpose flour

¾ cup whole-wheat flour

¾ cup sugar

1 tablespoon baking powder

2 egg whites

⅔ cup buttermilk

⅓ cup unsweetened applesauce

1 teaspoon almond extract

1 cup fresh raspberries

Preheat the oven to 400° F. Lightly coat a large muffin tin (six 3-inch-wide cups) with nonstick vegetable-oil spray.

In a large bowl, combine the flours, sugar, and baking powder and make a well in the center.

In a medium bowl, beat the egg whites until foamy; add the buttermilk, applesauce, and almond extract; add to the dry ingredients. Gently fold in the raspberries. Pour the batter into the prepared muffin cups.

Bake 22 to 25 minutes, or until light brown. Let cool 5 minutes, in pan, on a wire rack. Transfer muffins to the wire rack to cool completely.

Nancy's Eclairs

Makes 12 eclairs

❧❧ ❧❧ ❧❧ ❧❧

Once a year my neighbor Nancy makes her famous eclairs for her daughter's birthday, and I wait patiently and hopefully for leftovers. After you taste these, you'll know why this dessert gets chosen instead of a traditional birthday cake.

By the way, Nancy loves this made-over version and swears she can't tell the difference!

How fat and calories were lowered:

☛ Used light butter instead of regular butter in the pastry

☛ Replaced most of the whole eggs with egg whites in the pastry

☛ Used nonfat milk instead of whole milk in the filling

☛ Used cocoa powder instead of some of the chocolate chips in the frosting

☛ Used a combination of fat-free cream cheese and marshmallow creme in the icing instead of butter and egg yolks

Nutrition Scorecard (per serving)		
	Before	After
Calories	393	186
Fat (grams)	22	5
% calories from fat	48	26
Cholesterol (mg)	150	29

Pastry Puff

½ cup (1 stick) light butter

⅛ teaspoon salt

1 cup boiling water

1 cup all-purpose flour

1 whole egg

5 egg whites

Filling

2⅓ cups nonfat milk

1 (4.6-ounce) package cook-and-serve vanilla pudding (not instant)

Frosting

3 tablespoons chocolate chips

2 tablespoons marshmallow creme

2 tablespoons unsweetened cocoa powder

½ cup powdered sugar

2 ounces fat-free cream cheese

To make the pastry: In a medium saucepan, combine the light butter, salt, and water. Bring to a boil over medium-high heat, stirring occasionally. Remove from the heat.

Add flour and stir quickly with a wooden spoon. It looks rough at first but suddenly becomes smooth, at which point you stir faster. Let cool 10 minutes. Meanwhile, combine the whole egg and egg whites and beat thoroughly. Add the egg mixture, 2 tablespoons at a time, to the flour mixture, stirring after each addition, until the dough no longer looks slippery.

Preheat the oven to 400° F. Lightly coat two baking sheets with nonstick vegetable-oil spray.

Use a spoon or pastry bag to form the eclairs. Make 12 oblong shapes about 4 inches long. Bake for 10 minutes. Reduce the heat to 350° F. and bake about 25 minutes longer, or until dark golden and firm to the touch. Remove from the oven. Immediately slice horizontally with a sharp knife. Remove any soft dough from the inside. Let cool to room temperature before filling.

To make the filling: In a medium saucepan, combine the nonfat milk and pudding mix and cook, stirring, until bubbly. Remove from the heat. Cover and refrigerate until ready to use.

To make the icing: In a small microwavable bowl, melt the chocolate chips in the microwave, on High setting, stirring every 30 seconds. Stir in the marshmallow creme and set aside. In another small bowl, combine the cocoa powder and powdered sugar; set aside. In a medium bowl, beat together the fat-free cream cheese and about one-third of the cocoa powder mixture with an electric mixer on medium speed until creamy. Gradually beat in the remaining cocoa powder mixture. Add the melted chocolate chip mixture and mix until thoroughly blended. Frost the filled eclairs.

Healthy Homestyle Desserts

Raspberry Dapple Muffins

Nancy's Eclairs

Blueberry Buckle Bread

Apple Streusel Muffins

Glazed Lemon
Nut Bread

Easy Tiramisù

Chocolate Chip Muffins

Makes 6 large muffins

❊❊❊❊❊

These muffins are speckled with mini chocolate chips.
How fat and calories were lowered:

☞ Used fat-free sour cream instead of regular sour cream

☞ Reduced the amount of chocolate chips and replaced the regular-size chips with mini chips

☞ Replaced the butter with a combination of buttermilk and applesauce

☞ Used egg whites instead of whole eggs

Nutrition Scorecard *(per serving)*		
	Before	After
Calories	514	347
Fat (grams)	23	6
% calories from fat	40	15
Cholesterol (mg)	90	13

¾ cup whole-wheat flour

1 cup all-purpose flour

½ cup white sugar

¼ cup packed light brown sugar

1 tablespoon baking powder

2 egg whites

½ cup buttermilk

½ cup fat-free sour cream (containing no gelatin)

¼ cup unsweetened applesauce

½ teaspoon vanilla extract

½ cup mini chocolate chips

Preheat the oven to 400° F. Lightly coat 6 large, 3-inch muffin cups with nonstick vegetable-oil spray.

In a medium bowl, combine whole-wheat flour, all-purpose flour, white and brown sugars, and baking powder.

In a large bowl, beat the egg whites with an electric mixer until foamy. Stir in the buttermilk, fat-free sour cream, applesauce, and vanilla and mix until blended. Add flour mixture and mix by hand just until blended. Gently fold in mini chocolate chips.

Spoon the batter into the prepared muffin cups. Bake the muffins for 20 to 25 minutes, or until the tops are golden. Let cool, in pan, on a wire rack for 5 minutes. Remove muffins to the rack and let cool completely.

Tropical Macadamia Nut Bread

Serves 12

❦❦❦❦❦

This delightful bread gets its moistness from mashed bananas. Unlike most reduced-fat baked goods, this is even better the next day.

How fat and calories were lowered:

- Reduced the amount of macadamia nuts
- Reduced the amount of coconut
- Eliminated the butter and replaced it with extra mashed bananas

Nutrition Scorecard
(per serving)

	Before	After
Calories	313	210
Fat (grams)	17	6
% calories from fat	48	25
Cholesterol (mg)	56	0

1 cup whole-wheat flour

1 cup all-purpose flour

¾ cup sugar

1 tablespoon finely grated orange zest

1 teaspoon baking soda

4 egg whites

1¼ cups mashed ripe bananas
    (about 3 medium)

¼ cup fresh orange juice

⅔ cup flaked coconut

½ cup coarsely chopped macadamia nuts
    or walnuts

Preheat the oven to 350° F. Lightly coat a 9x5x3-inch loaf pan with nonstick vegetable-oil spray.

In a medium bowl, combine the whole-wheat flour, all-purpose flour, sugar, orange zest, and baking soda.

In a large bowl, beat the egg whites with an electric mixer until foamy. Add the mashed bananas and orange juice and beat until blended. Add flour mixture and beat until blended. By hand, fold in the coconut and nuts. Pour the batter into the prepared pan.

Bake 50 to 55 minutes, or until a toothpick inserted near the center comes out clean. Let cool 10 minutes, in the pan, on a wire rack. Remove the bread from the pan and let cool completely on the rack.

Glazed Lemon Nut Bread

Serves 12

❧❧ ❧❧ ❧❧

The fresh lemon glaze makes the zesty lemon flavor of this bread come alive.

How fat and calories were lowered:

☞ Used applesauce instead of butter

☞ Replaced whole eggs with egg whites

☞ Replaced regular sour cream with fat-free sour cream

☞ Reduced the amount of nuts

Nutrition Scorecard *(per serving)*		
	Before	After
Calories	309	187
Fat (grams)	16	4
% calories from fat	45	17
Cholesterol (mg)	61	0

Lemon Bread

1 ½ cups all-purpose flour

1 cup sugar

½ cup whole-wheat flour

1 tablespoon finely grated lemon zest

2 teaspoons baking powder

¼ cup fresh lemon juice

¼ cup unsweetened applesauce

4 egg whites

½ cup fat-free sour cream (containing no gelatin)

½ cup chopped pecans or walnuts

Lemon Glaze

½ cup sifted powdered sugar

1 tablespoon fresh lemon juice

¼ teaspoon finely grated lemon zest

Preheat the oven to 350° F. Lightly coat a 9x5x3-inch loaf pan with nonstick vegetable-oil spray.

To make the bread: In a medium bowl, combine the all-purpose flour, sugar, whole-wheat flour, lemon zest, and baking powder. In a small bowl, combine the lemon juice and applesauce.

In a large bowl, beat the egg whites with an electric mixer until foamy. Add the fat-free sour cream and beat until blended. Add the lemon juice mixture and continue beating. Add the flour mixture and stir by hand until blended. Fold in the pecans. Pour the batter into the prepared pan.

Bake 50 to 55 minutes, or until a toothpick inserted near the center comes out clean. Let cool, in the pan, on a wire rack for 10 minutes. Remove from the pan and let cool completely on the rack. Ice with the lemon glaze.

To make the lemon glaze: In a small bowl, combine the powdered sugar, lemon juice, and lemon zest. Stir until smooth.

Lemons Are Rich in Vitamin C

Just ¼ cup of fresh lemon juice provides 28 milligrams of vitamin C, nearly half of the Recommended Dietary Allowance for adult nonsmokers.

❝❞❝❞❝❞

Peach Pecan Crumb Muffins

Makes 6 large muffins

⚜ ⚜ ⚜ ⚜ ⚜

These homey muffins are crowned extra-special with a pecan topping. How fat and calories were lowered:

Topping

☞ Reduced the amount of pecans

☞ Replaced regular butter with light butter

Muffins

☞ Used a combination of applesauce and buttermilk instead of oil

Nutrition Scorecard *(per serving)*	Before	After
Calories	512	313
Fat (grams)	28	5
% calories from fat	47	15
Cholesterol (mg)	89	5

Pecan Crumb Topping

⅓ cup chopped pecans

⅓ cup packed light brown sugar

3 tablespoons all-purpose flour

1 teaspoon cinnamon

1½ tablespoons light butter, melted

Muffins

1 cup all-purpose flour

½ cup whole-wheat flour

½ cup sugar

2 teaspoons baking powder

1 teaspoon cinnamon

2 egg whites

½ cup buttermilk

¼ cup unsweetened applesauce

1 cup finely diced peeled peaches

(about 1 large peach)

To make the topping: In a small bowl, combine pecans, the brown sugar, the 3 tablespoons all-purpose flour, and the 1 teaspoon cinnamon. Add the melted light butter and stir until mixture is crumbly.

To make the muffins: Preheat the oven to 400° F. Spray a large muffin tin (six 3-inch-wide cups) with nonstick vegetable-oil spray. In a large bowl, combine the 1 cup all-purpose flour, the whole-wheat flour, the sugar, the baking powder, and the 1 teaspoon cinnamon; make a well in the center.

In a small bowl, beat the egg whites until foamy; add the buttermilk and applesauce. Add to the dry ingredients. Gently fold in the peaches. Pour the batter into the prepared muffin cups. Sprinkle the topping over the batter.

Bake 18 to 22 minutes, or until light brown. Let cool 5 minutes, in pan, on a wire rack. Transfer the muffins to the rack and let cool completely.

Milk

Contrary to popular belief, calcium does not get stripped away when the fat is removed. In fact, nonfat milk is slightly higher in calcium:

1 cup	Calcium content (mg)
skim milk	302
lowfat milk	297
whole milk	291

Cranberry Citrus Bundt Bread (Fat-Free, Too)

Serves 12

✄✄✄✄✄

This recipe started off as a muffin, but it grew into this delightful bread—one of my favorites. I am usually the first to defend keeping nuts in a recipe, because they impart a unique flavor and texture that would otherwise be missed. This bread is an exception. I substituted dried cranberries for the nuts and they worked beautifully.

How fat and calories were lowered:

☛ Used nonfat yogurt instead of butter and sour cream

☛ Eliminated nuts as described above

☛ Replaced whole egg with egg whites

Nutrition Scorecard (per serving)	Before	After
Calories	380	189
Fat (grams)	19	0
% calories from fat	44	1
Cholesterol (mg)	30	0

Bread

½ cup dried cranberries

⅓ cup fresh orange juice

1 medium orange, washed

1 cup fresh cranberries, rinsed and sorted

1 cup all-purpose flour

1 cup sugar

¾ cup whole-wheat flour

2 teaspoons baking powder

1 cup nonfat vanilla yogurt

1 teaspoon baking soda

2 egg whites

Citrus Glaze

½ cup powdered sugar

5 teaspoons fresh orange juice

Preheat the oven to 375° F. Lightly coat a fluted tube pan with nonstick vegetable-oil spray.

In a small bowl, combine the dried cranberries and orange juice.

Cut the orange into 8 small pieces. Place the orange pieces and fresh cranberries in a food processor or blender. Pulse until coarsely chopped.

In a medium bowl, combine the all-purpose flour, sugar, whole-wheat flour, and baking powder.

In a large bowl, stir together the yogurt and baking soda. (The volume will nearly double.) Using an electric mixer, beat in the egg whites one at a time. Beat in the chopped orange mixture. Add the dried cranberry mixture and beat until blended. Add flour mixture and beat just until combined. Transfer the batter to the prepared pan. Bake 40 to 45 minutes, or until a wooden toothpick inserted near the center comes out clean. Remove from oven. Invert and cool 10 minutes on a wire rack (bread will still be clinging to pan). Gently run a knife around the outer edges and remove the bread. Let it cool completely on the rack and glaze when cool.

To make the glaze: In a small bowl, stir together the powdered sugar and orange juice until smooth. Drizzle evenly over the cooled bread.

Glazed Poppy Seed Bread (Fat-Free, Too)

Makes 2 loaves, 12 slices each

⨯⨯ ⨯⨯ ⨯⨯ ⨯⨯ ⨯⨯

This recipe makes two loaves—share one with a friend or freeze it for a future treat.

How fat and calories were lowered:

☞ Substituted applesauce for oil and incorporated buttermilk for added body

☞ Replaced whole eggs with egg whites

☞ Reduced the amount of sugar

☞ Incorporated whole-wheat flour for added nutrition

Nutrition Scorecard
(per slice)

	Before	After
Calories	260	144
Fat (grams)	12	0
% calories from fat	42	0
Cholesterol (mg)	57	0

Poppy Seed Bread

1½ cups whole-wheat flour (do not
  substitute)

1½ cups all-purpose flour

2 cups sugar

1½ teaspoons baking powder

¼ teaspoon salt

6 egg whites

1 cup unsweetened applesauce

1½ cups buttermilk

1½ teaspoons vanilla extract

1½ teaspoons almond extract

1½ teaspoons imitation butter flavor

1 teaspoon finely grated orange zest

4 teaspoons poppy seeds

Orange Glaze

⅓ cup powdered sugar

2 tablespoons fresh orange juice

¼ teaspoon almond extract

¼ teaspoon vanilla extract

¼ teaspoon imitation butter flavor

Preheat the oven to 350° F. Lightly coat two 9x5x3-inch loaf pans with nonstick vegetable-oil spray.

To make the bread: In a large bowl, stir together the whole-wheat flour, all-purpose flour, sugar, baking powder, and salt. Make a well in the center of the mixture.

In another large bowl, beat the egg whites until foamy. Stir in the applesauce, buttermilk, vanilla, almond extract, butter flavor, orange zest, and poppy seeds.

Add the egg white mixture to the flour mixture and stir until just blended. Fold the batter into the prepared pans. Bake for 55 to 65 minutes, or until golden. Let the bread cool, in the pans, on a wire rack, for 10 minutes, then remove the bread and drizzle the top with the glaze. Let cool completely on the rack before slicing.

To make the glaze: In a small bowl, combine the powdered sugar, orange juice, almond and vanilla extracts, and butter flavor. Stir until smooth.

Healthy Homestyle Desserts

Decadent

Cakes

Easy Tiramisù

Serves 12

✕✕ ✕✕ ✕✕ ✕✕

This incredibly simple recipe was inspired by a story told to me by a couple while I finished off dinner with my all-time favorite dessert, tiramisù.

Lou and Maria honeymooned in Italy, where Lou has family. During their travels they stopped and visited four different sets of relatives over a period of one day. Each family, unbeknownst to the others, made tiramisù as a special tribute for the American visitors. Not to offend their gracious hosts, the honeymooners accepted each and every generous portion of tiramisù. By their last visit, they weren't feeling so well. As you might imagine, to this day Lou and Maria do not look as fondly as I do upon this rich Italian delight.

When Lou finished telling his tiramisù story, I begged to get an authentic recipe from his Italian family. To my delight, I received such a recipe through his cousin Roberta, who lives in Vasto, Italy. The one thing she insists on is that whatever you do, you must use mascarpone, the Italian cheese, for which there is truly no comparable substitute. She must be right, because I have tasted "light" tiramisù, in which there is no mascarpone, and it's just not the same. It's well worth the effort to track down this slightly sweet Italian cream cheese, which can be found in specialty cheese stores, gourmet shops, and Italian delis.

How fat and calories were lowered:

❧ Used a fat-free sponge cake in place of Savoiardi (lady fingers)

❧ Reduced the amount of mascarpone cheese and replaced it in part with fat-free ricotta

❧ Used light nondairy whipped topping instead of whipping cream

Nutrition Scorecard (per serving)		
	Before	After
Calories	412	232
Fat (grams)	34	10
% calories from fat	71	43
Cholesterol (mg)	150	24

8 ounces mascarpone cheese
½ cup powdered sugar
½ cup fat-free ricotta cheese
¾ cup thawed frozen light nondairy whipped topping

¾ cup freshly brewed espresso or other strong coffee
¼ cup coffee liqueur
1 (14-ounce) loaf fat-free golden cake
2 teaspoons unsweetened cocoa powder

In a large bowl, beat together the mascarpone and powdered sugar with an electric mixer on low speed until just blended. Using a rubber spatula, fold in the fat-free ricotta cheese. Fold in the whipped topping.

In a small bowl, combine the espresso and liqueur.

Using a long serrated knife, cut the loaf cake horizontally into 8 thin slices. (Don't worry if there is breakage; you can easily piece crumbs and remnants into this dessert.)

To assemble: Arrange half the sliced cake pieces in a 10x10-inch pan, covering entire bottom. Using a pastry brush, drizzle half of the coffee mixture evenly over the bottom cake layer. Gently add a layer of the mascarpone cheese mixture, distributing evenly. Repeat layering with remaining cake, coffee mixture, and mascarpone mixture. Sprinkle or sift the cocoa powder over the top mascarpone layer. Cover and chill at least 2 hours. (This tastes even better if you let it chill overnight.) Cut into 12 pieces and serve.

Ricotta Cheese

Ricotta cheese is a good source of calcium. One-half cup provides 334 milligrams of calcium, more calcium than in one cup of milk.

✄ ✄ ✄ ✄ ✄

Lemon Intensity Bundt Cake

Serves 12

꿹 꿹 꿹 꿹 꿹

This is my favorite lemon cake. It's spiked with a fresh lemon juice marinade on the inside and gets crowned with a zesty lemon glaze on top. Tip: As irresistible as this cake is, be sure to let it cool completely as directed or it will crumble when sliced. It tastes best after standing overnight.

How fat and calories were lowered:

☞ Replaced oil with a combination of applesauce and buttermilk

☞ Used egg whites instead of whole eggs and beat them until foamy for extra tenderness

Nutrition Scorecard		
(per serving)		
	Before	*After*
Calories	429	288
Fat (grams)	19	4
% calories from fat	41	12
Cholesterol (mg)	71	1

Lemon Cake

6 egg whites

1⅓ cups buttermilk

⅓ cup unsweetened applesauce

1 (18¼-ounce) box (2-layer) lemon
    cake mix

1 (3-ounce) package regular lemon gelatin

2 teaspoons finely grated lemon zest

Lemon Marinade

1 cup powdered sugar

⅓ cup fresh lemon juice

Lemon Glaze

¾ cup powdered sugar

5 teaspoons fresh lemon juice

1½ teaspoons finely grated lemon zest

To make the cake: Preheat the oven to 350° F. Lightly coat a 12-cup Bundt pan with nonstick vegetable-oil spray.

In a large bowl, beat the egg whites with an electric mixer at high speed for 1 minute (they will triple in volume). Add the buttermilk and beat until blended. Beat in the applesauce. Add the cake mix, the gelatin, and the 2 teaspoons lemon zest and beat on medium speed for 2 minutes. Spread the batter in the prepared pan.

Bake for 35 minutes, or until the cake springs back when lightly touched in the center.

While the cake is baking, prepare the marinade. Remove the cake from the oven and place it, in the pan, on a wire rack (do not invert). Use a toothpick to poke deep holes (about ⅛ inch apart) evenly across the cake and pour the marinade over the hot cake.

Let cake cool completely while still in pan. After cake is cool, gently loosen the sides of the pan with a knife. Invert the pan and remove the cake. Place the cake on a plate and glaze it.

To make the lemon marinade: In a small bowl, stir together the 1 cup powdered sugar and the ⅓ cup lemon juice until smooth. Use as directed above.

To make the lemon glaze: In a small bowl, stir together the ¾ cup powdered sugar, the 5 teaspoons lemon juice, and the 1½ teaspoons lemon zest. Slowly drizzle half the glaze evenly on top of cake. Let set about 5 minutes and drizzle remaining glaze.

Triple-Layer German Chocolate Cake

Serves 12

❧❧❧❧❧

This show-stopping cake is a breeze to make. With a frosting this good, you need three layers to show it off.

How fat and calories were lowered:

In the cake

☞ Replaced oil with baby-food prunes

☞ Used egg whites instead of whole eggs

In the frosting

☞ Used cornstarch for thickening instead of egg yolk

☞ Used evaporated skim milk instead of regular milk

☞ Used light butter instead of regular butter

☞ Reduced the amount of coconut and pecans, and toasted the pecans to help bring out the rich nutty flavor without the extra fat and calories

Nutrition Scorecard *(per serving)*		
	Before	After
Calories	533	399
Fat (grams)	31	14
% calories from fat	53	31
Cholesterol (mg)	133	11

Chocolate Cake

6 egg whites

1¼ cups buttermilk

2 (2½-ounce) jars baby-food prunes

1 (18¼-ounce) box (2-layer) German chocolate cake mix

Pecan Coconut Frosting

¾ cup sugar

2 tablespoons cornstarch

½ cup light butter

¼ cup light corn syrup

1 cup evaporated skim milk

1 teaspoon vanilla extract

¾ cup flaked coconut

⅔ cup chopped pecans, toasted

Preheat the oven to 350° F. Lightly coat three 9-inch round cake pans with nonstick vegetable-oil spray; then line with wax paper. Spray wax paper with nonstick spray.

To make the chocolate cake: In a large bowl, beat the egg whites with an electric mixer at high speed for 1 minute (they will triple in volume). Add the buttermilk and beat until blended. Beat in the baby-food prunes. Add the cake mix and beat on medium speed for 2 minutes. Pour the batter into the prepared pans.

Healthy Homestyle Desserts

Bake 15 to 20 minutes, until cake springs back when lightly touched in the center. Cool completely, in the pans, on a wire rack. Carefully remove the cakes from the pans. Invert the first layer on a cake platter. Spread one-third of the pecan frosting over the entire layer. Add the second cake layer, rounded side down. Frost with half of the remaining frosting. Add the last cake layer, rounded side down. Add the remaining frosting.

To make the frosting: In a small bowl, mix together the sugar and cornstarch. In a medium saucepan, melt the light butter. Add the corn syrup, sugar mixture, and evaporated skim milk. Cook and stir over medium heat until bubbly. Cook and stir one additional minute. Remove from the heat. Let cool 15 minutes. Stir in vanilla, coconut, and toasted pecans.

How to Make Your Own Prune Puree

In a food processor, combine 8 ounces (1⅓ cups) pitted prunes with 6 tablespoons hot water. Blend until smooth. Makes 1 cup. To store, cover and refrigerate up to one month.

Source: California Prune Board.

✂ ✂ ✂ ✂ ✂

Hawaiian Mandarin Cake

Serves 12

❦❦❦❦❦

Thiis refreshing cake is ideal in warm weather.
How fat and calories were lowered:

🍃 Replaced vegetable oil with applesauce

🍃 Used egg whites instead of whole eggs

🍃 Replaced half the whipped topping with nonfat vanilla yogurt

🍃 Used mandarin oranges packed in juice rather than syrup

Nutrition Scorecard		
(per serving)		
	Before	*After*
Calories	372	283
Fat (grams)	16	5
% calories from fat	40	17
Cholesterol (mg)	36	0

Mandarin Orange Cake

4 egg whites

*1 (11-ounce) can mandarin oranges
(juice-packed), juice reserved*

½ cup buttermilk

½ cup unsweetened applesauce

*1 (18¼-ounce) box (2-layer) lemon
cake mix*

Pineapple Cream Topping

*1 (8-ounce) can crushed pineapple,
undrained (juice-packed)*

8 ounces nonfat vanilla yogurt

*1 small package (3.4-ounce) instant
vanilla pudding mix*

*1½ cups thawed frozen light nondairy
whipped topping*

Preheat the oven to 350° F. Lightly coat a 13x9x2-inch baking pan with nonstick vegetable-oil spray.

In a large bowl, beat the egg whites with an electric mixer on high speed for 1 minute. Add the reserved mandarin orange juice, buttermilk, and applesauce and beat until blended. Add the cake mix and beat on medium speed 2 minutes. Pour the batter into the prepared pan. Distribute the mandarin oranges evenly on top of the batter.

Bake 30 to 35 minutes, until cake springs back when touched lightly in the center, or until toothpick inserted near center comes out clean. Let cool completely, in the pan, on a wire rack.

To make the topping: In a medium bowl, combine the crushed pineapple (with juice) and yogurt. Add the pudding mix and beat until thickened, about 60 seconds. Fold in the light whipped topping. Spread the pineapple topping on the cooled cake and serve straight from the pan. Store covered in refrigerator.

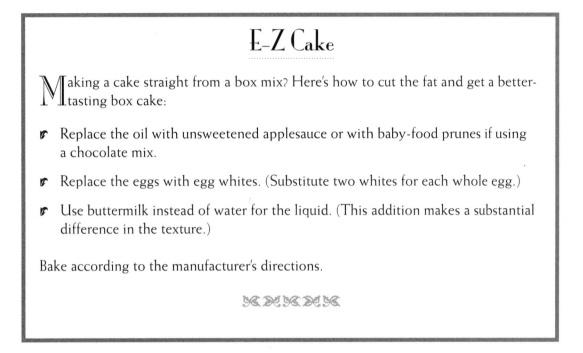

E-Z Cake

Making a cake straight from a box mix? Here's how to cut the fat and get a better-tasting box cake:

🐦 Replace the oil with unsweetened applesauce or with baby-food prunes if using a chocolate mix.

🐦 Replace the eggs with egg whites. (Substitute two whites for each whole egg.)

🐦 Use buttermilk instead of water for the liquid. (This addition makes a substantial difference in the texture.)

Bake according to the manufacturer's directions.

Pumpkin Pudding Cake

Serves 16

✄ ✄ ✄ ✄

This unusual dessert is a cross between pumpkin pie and pumpkin cake, with a pudding on the bottom and a thin cake layer on top. This is fast and easy to make.

How fat and calories were lowered:

☞ Used egg whites instead of whole eggs

☞ Used evaporated skim milk instead of whole milk

☞ Used a single-layer rather than a double-layer cake mix

☞ Reduced amount of pecans

☞ Used a brown sugar glaze instead of a butter glaze

Nutrition Scorecard
(per serving)

	Before	After
Calories	353	220
Fat (grams)	18	5
% calories from fat	45	20
Cholesterol (mg)	80	0

---

1 (29-ounce) can pumpkin (not pie filling)

8 egg whites

1 (12-ounce) can evaporated skim milk

¾ cup sugar

1 teaspoon cinnamon

1 teaspoon ground ginger

½ teaspoon ground cloves

½ teaspoon ground nutmeg

1 (9-ounce) package (single-layer) yellow cake mix

¾ cup chopped pecans

Glaze

¾ cup packed light brown sugar

¼ cup hot water

Preheat the oven to 325° F. Lightly coat a 9x13-inch baking pan with nonstick vegetable-oil spray.

In a large mixing bowl, beat together the pumpkin puree and egg whites with an electric mixer on medium speed. Add the evaporated skim milk, sugar, cinnamon, ginger, cloves, and nutmeg and beat until smooth. Transfer the batter to the prepared pan. Sprinkle the dry cake mix evenly over the batter. Sprinkle the pecans over the cake mix layer.

In a small bowl, combine the brown sugar and hot water.

Drizzle the brown sugar mixture over the pecan layer. Cover with aluminum foil. Bake 1 hour, then remove foil and bake an additional 15 minutes.

Orange Sunshine Cake

Serves 12

⋈⋈ ⋈⋈ ⋈⋈ ⋈

This pretty cake tastes especially fresh with the orange zest in both the cake and the frosting. The frosting tends to crack if left out too long, so be sure either to cover the frosted cake or to wait until the last possible moment to frost it.

How fat and calories were lowered:

Cake

- Reduced amount of sugar slightly
- Used egg whites instead of whole eggs
- Replaced shortening with unsweetened applesauce
- Used buttermilk instead of whole milk

Frosting

- Reduced the amount of nuts
- Used fat-free cream cheese instead of shortening and butter
- Added orange zest to enhance flavor
- Used nonfat milk for the pudding base instead of whole milk

Nutrition Scorecard (per serving)		
	Before	After
Calories	524	256
Fat (grams)	34	4
% calories from fat	57	16
Cholesterol (mg)	61	4

Cake

2 cups all-purpose flour

1⅓ cups sugar, divided use

2 teaspoons baking powder

¼ teaspoon baking soda

4 egg whites

¾ cup buttermilk

¼ cup fresh orange juice

½ cup unsweetened applesauce

1 tablespoon finely grated orange zest

Frosting

8 ounces fat-free cream cheese

3 tablespoons fresh orange juice

¾ cup nonfat milk

1 small (3.4-ounce) package instant fat-free vanilla pudding

1 tablespoon finely grated orange zest

⅔ cup finely chopped walnuts

Preheat the oven to 350° F. Lightly coat two 8-inch round cake pans with nonstick vegetable-oil spray. Line with wax paper and lightly coat the wax paper with nonstick spray.

To make the cake: In a large bowl, combine flour, 1 cup of the sugar, baking powder, and baking soda.

In a large bowl, beat the egg whites with an electric beater on high speed until foamy. Gradually add the remaining ⅓ cup sugar and beat until stiff peaks form. Set aside.

Add the buttermilk, the ¼ cup orange juice, the applesauce, and the 1 tablespoon orange zest to the flour mixture. Beat on medium speed until blended. Using a rubber spatula, fold in the beaten egg whites. Transfer the batter to the prepared cake pans.

Bake about 25 minutes, or until the cake springs back when pressed lightly in the center. Let cool, in the pans, 10 minutes on a wire rack, then carefully remove the cakes. Let the layers cool on the rack.

To make the frosting: In a small bowl, beat the cream cheese with an electric mixer on low speed until smooth. Gradually add the 3 tablespoons orange juice while continuing to beat.

In a medium bowl, beat together the nonfat milk and pudding mix for 2 minutes on low speed. Fold in the cream cheese mixture, the remaining 1 tablespoon orange zest, and the walnuts. Spread about one-third of the frosting between the cake layers. Frost the top and sides of the cake with the remaining frosting.

Krystin's Fantasy Fudge Cake

Serves 12

✕✕✕✕✕

Every year my daughter makes her customary request for a special birthday cake. But on her seventh birthday she wanted both homemade fudge and a chocolate cake. In her honor I created this cake, which is filled with a lower-fat fudge icing instead of a rich ganache. The guests went crazy and even suggested names such as "Un-Death by Chocolate Cake," because while the chocolate richness is to die for, its lower-fat nature doesn't leave you feeling slothlike.

How fat and calories were lowered:

Nutrition Scorecard *(per serving)*	Before	After
Calories	967	414
Fat (grams)	62	12
% calories from fat	55	25
Cholesterol (mg)	162	1

Cake:

- Replaced oil with baby-food prunes
- Used buttermilk for added body
- Replaced whole eggs with egg whites
- Reduced the amount of almonds, and switched to sliced. (Sliced almonds cover more surface area with fewer calories than chopped.)

Frosting:

- Used a commercial fat-free fudge topping for one layer
- Reduced the amount of chocolate chips
- Replaced the butter with baby-food prunes
- Used marshmallow creme instead of heavy cream

Cake

6 egg whites

1⅓ cups buttermilk

2 (2½-ounce) jars baby-food prunes

1 (18¼-ounce) box (2-layer) chocolate
    cake mix

Frosting and Filling

½ cup fat-free fudge topping

1 cup marshmallow creme

1 cup chocolate chips, melted

1 (2½-ounce) jar baby-food prunes

¼ cup finely chopped walnuts

⅓ cup sliced almonds

Preheat the oven to 350° F. Lightly coat three 9-inch round cake pans with nonstick vegetable-oil spray, then line with wax paper. Spray wax paper with nonstick spray.

To make the cake: In a large bowl, beat the egg whites with an electric mixer at high speed for 1 minute (they will triple in volume). Add the buttermilk and beat until blended. Beat in the baby-food prunes. Add the cake mix and beat on medium speed for 2 minutes. Pour the batter into the prepared pans.

Bake 15 to 20 minutes, until cake springs back when lightly touched in the center. Let cool, in the pans, on a wire rack.

To make frosting and assemble: Remove cake from pans. Frost first layer with fat-free fudge topping. Place second cake layer, rounded side down, over fudge topping layer.

Mix together the marshmallow creme and melted chocolate chips until smooth. Stir in the baby-food prunes. Combine one-third of the marshmallow creme mixture with the chopped walnuts and spread over the second cake layer. Place last cake layer, rounded side down, over the walnut mixture. Frost the top and sides of the cake with the remaining marshmallow mixture.

Carefully place each almond slice flatly on the side of the cake. Continue until the sides are covered.

Healthy Homestyle Desserts

Chocolate Zucchini Snack Cake

Serves 12

✠ ✠ ✠ ✠

This moist cake already has a "frosting" built in and is perfect for a last-minute potluck. You can also cut this cake into small pieces for a nice little lunch box surprise.

How fat and calories were lowered:

✞ Replaced butter with applesauce

✞ Reduced oil substantially and compensated by increasing buttermilk

✞ Reduced the amount of nuts

✞ Used mini chocolate chips (and less of them) in place of regular-size chips

✞ Replaced whole eggs with egg whites

✞ Reduced the amount of sugar

Nutrition Scorecard		
(per serving)		
	Before	*After*
Calories	495	300
Fat *(grams)*	28	9
% calories from fat	49	24
Cholesterol *(mg)*	57	0

2¼ cups all-purpose flour

1½ cups sugar

½ cup unsweetened cocoa powder

1 teaspoon baking soda

¼ teaspoon salt

¾ cup buttermilk

½ cup unsweetened applesauce

1 tablespoon oil (preferably canola)

1 teaspoon vanilla extract

4 egg whites

2 cups grated unpeeled zucchini
   (about 2½ medium)

⅔ cup mini chocolate chips

½ cup chopped walnuts

Preheat the oven to 325° F. Lightly coat a 9x13-inch baking pan with nonstick vegetable-oil spray.

In a large bowl, combine the flour, sugar, cocoa, baking soda, and salt.

In a medium bowl, combine the buttermilk, applesauce, oil, and vanilla.

In another large bowl, beat the egg whites with an electric mixer on high speed for 1 minute. Add buttermilk mixture and beat until blended.

Combine egg white mixture and flour mixture and beat until blended. Mix in the grated zucchini and ⅓ cup of the chocolate chips. Pour the batter into the prepared pan. Sprinkle the remaining chocolate chips and the nuts over the batter.

Bake about 50 minutes, or until a toothpick inserted near the center comes out clean. Let the cake cool completely, in the pan, on a wire rack.

White Chocolate vs. Milk or Dark Chocolate

Both chocolates are comparable in fat and colories, but milk and dark chocolate are much lower in saturated fat. White chocolate is usually made with palm kernel oil, a highly saturated fat. Palm kernel oil is 81 percent saturated fat, double the saturated fat content of lard!

✄ ✄ ✄ ✄ ✄

Maple Pecan Coffee Cake

Serves 12

⊁ ⊁ ⊁ ⊁ ⊁

A wonderful treat to serve with brunch.
How fat and calories were lowered:

Cake:

☛ Used a combination of buttermilk and canola oil in place of butter

☛ Reduced the amount of pecans

☛ Replaced the whole eggs with egg whites

Glaze:

☛ Replaced the butter with light butter and used much less of it

☛ Used nonfat milk instead of cream

Nutrition Scorecard *(per serving)*		
	Before	*After*
Calories	519	290
Fat (grams)	40	8
% calories from fat	68	25
Cholesterol (mg)	154	1

Cake

¾ cup coarsely chopped pecans, toasted

2¼ cups all-purpose flour

1 teaspoon baking powder

⅛ teaspoon salt

9 egg whites

1 cup sugar

½ cup pure maple syrup

¼ cup buttermilk

2 tablespoons oil (preferably canola)

1 teaspoon maple extract

Glaze

½ cup powdered sugar

1 tablespoon light butter, melted

1 teaspoon pure maple syrup

1 teaspoon maple extract

1 teaspoon nonfat milk

Preheat the oven to 350° F. Lightly coat a 12-cup Bundt pan with nonstick vegetable-oil spray.

To make the cake: Finely grind the pecans in a food processor or blender. In a large bowl, combine ground pecans, flour, baking powder, and salt.

In another large bowl, beat the egg whites with an electric mixer on high speed until foamy. Gradually beat in the 1 cup sugar. Beat until soft peaks form and set aside.

In a small bowl, combine the ½ cup maple syrup, the buttermilk, the oil, and the 1 teaspoon maple extract. Add maple mixture to flour mixture. Using an electric mixer on medium speed, beat until blended. Add half of the egg white mixture and beat until blended. Fold in the remaining egg whites. Pour into the prepared pan.

Bake 45 to 50 minutes, or until the top is golden and a toothpick inserted near the center comes out clean.

Invert the pan (with cake still in pan) on rack and let cool 10 minutes. With a small knife, cut around sides and center of pan to loosen cake. Turn cake out onto rack and let cool completely.

To make the glaze: In a small bowl, combine the powdered sugar, the melted light butter, the 1 teaspoon maple syrup, 1 teaspoon maple extract, and the nonfat milk. Stir until smooth and drizzle over cooled cake.

Pineapple Upside-Down Cake

Serves 8

⋈ ⋈ ⋈ ⋈

This is one of my husband's favorite cakes, and there's only 1 gram of fat per serving.

How fat and calories were lowered:

Topping:

☞ Reduced amount of butter

☞ Reduced amount of brown sugar

Cake

☞ Used applesauce instead of butter

☞ Replaced whole eggs with egg whites

Nutrition Scorecard *(per serving)*		
	Before	After
Calories	374	247
Fat (grams)	14	1
% calories from fat	34	4
Cholesterol (mg)	63	3

Pineapple Topping

1 (20-ounce) can crushed pineapple
    (juice-packed), juice reserved

2 teaspoons butter, melted

½ cup packed light brown sugar

Cake

1¼ cups all-purpose flour

⅔ cup sugar

1½ teaspoons baking powder

¼ teaspoon ground ginger

⅛ teaspoon salt

2 egg whites

⅔ cup pineapple juice (reserved from can)

⅓ cup unsweetened applesauce

1 teaspoon vanilla extract

Preheat the oven to 350° F. Lightly coat a 9-inch round cake pan with nonstick vegetable-oil spray.

To make the topping: Squeeze the excess juice from the crushed pineapple and pat the pineapple dry (or you will end up with a soggy cake). Drizzle the melted butter over the bottom of the prepared pan. Sprinkle the brown sugar over the bottom of the pan. Add the crushed pineapple evenly over the brown sugar. Set aside.

To make the cake: In a large bowl, combine the flour, sugar, baking powder, ginger, and salt. In another large bowl, beat the egg whites until soft peaks form. Gradually beat in the pineapple juice, applesauce, and vanilla until blended. Combine the egg white mixture with the flour mixture and beat until blended. Pour the batter over the crushed pineapple.

Bake 40 to 45 minutes, or until a toothpick inserted near the center comes out clean. Let cool, in the pan, on a wire rack for 5 minutes. Loosen the cake around the edges. Invert onto a serving platter.

How Sweet Is Your Food?

Want to know how much sugar is in your morning cereal or other foods? Check out the food label. It lists the grams of sugar per serving. Each 4 grams of sugar is equal to one teaspoon. For example, one 12-ounce cola has 36 grams of sugar, or 9 teaspoons.

✄ ✄ ✄ ✄ ✄

Cappuccino Raspberry Cake

Serves 12

⨯⨯⨯⨯⨯

This dense cake is heavenly, rich, and moist.
How fat and calories were lowered:

Cake:

☞ Used applesauce in place of some of the oil

☞ Used fat-free sour cream instead of regular sour cream

☞ Replaced whole eggs with egg whites

☞ Added buttermilk with instant coffee granules instead of brewed coffee to add body

☞ Replaced part of the baking chocolate squares with cocoa

☞ Reduced the amount of sugar

Frosting:

☞ Used fat-free fudge topping instead of regular cream cheese

☞ Reduced the amount of chocolate chips

Nutrition Scorecard *(per serving)*	Before	After
Calories	573	333
Fat (grams)	24	6
% calories from fat	35	15
Cholesterol (mg)	48	1

Cappuccino Cake

1¾ cups sugar

1½ cups all-purpose flour

⅓ cup unsweetened cocoa powder

¾ teaspoon baking soda

2 ounces unsweetened baking chocolate, melted

1 teaspoon oil (preferably canola)

5 teaspoons instant coffee granules

1 cup buttermilk

½ cup unsweetened applesauce

½ cup fat-free sour cream (containing no gelatin)

4 egg whites

Raspberry Filling

½ cup seedless raspberry jam

2 tablespoons semisweet chocolate chips, melted

Chocolate Frosting

1 teaspoon instant coffee granules

1 tablespoon nonfat milk

1 cup fat-free fudge topping

⅓ cup semisweet chocolate chips

Preheat the oven to 350° F. Lightly coat three 8-inch round cake pans with nonstick vegetable-oil spray.

To make the cake: In a large bowl, combine the sugar, flour, cocoa powder, and baking soda. In a small bowl or cup, combine the melted baking chocolate and oil. In another small bowl, dissolve the 5 teaspoons instant coffee granules in the buttermilk. Add the applesauce and sour cream.

In a large mixing bowl, beat the egg whites with an electric mixer on high speed until soft peaks form. Add the buttermilk mixture and beat until blended. Add half the flour mixture and beat until combined. Add remaining flour mixture and beat until combined. Drizzle in the melted chocolate mixture and beat until blended. Pour the batter into the prepared cake pans.

Bake 25 to 30 minutes, or until a toothpick inserted near the center comes out clean. Let cool 10 minutes on a wire rack and then remove cake from pans.

To assemble the filling: If you frost while the cake is still warm, it spreads and melds better. Invert first layer on cake platter. Spread half of the raspberry jam evenly over the cake layer. Drizzle 1 tablespoon of the melted chocolate chips over entire layer. Add the second cake layer, rounded side down, and repeat with the remaining preserves and the remaining tablespoon melted chocolate chips. Add the last cake layer, rounded side down.

To make the frosting: In a medium microwavable bowl, dissolve 1 teaspoon instant coffee granules in the milk. Add the fudge topping and chocolate chips. Microwave on High for 30 seconds, stir well. Repeat until the frosting is smooth and all the chocolate chips are melted. While the frosting is still warm, ice the top and sides of the cake.

Cinnamon Streusel Coffee Cake

Hawaiian Mandarin Cake

Almost Fat-Free Cheesecake

Carrot Spice Cake

Serves 12

✖✖✖✖✖

Ihere are some recipes that just get better the more you fiddle with them, and this is one of them. The cake itself is actually fat-free, but I cannot imagine a carrot cake without a good cream cheese frosting. In this frosting, fat-free cream cheese will just not do, but the light tub-style cream cheese is terrific and still lower in fat than regular cream cheese.

How fat and calories were lowered:

☞ Eliminated nuts

☞ Used egg whites instead of whole eggs

☞ Replaced oil with a combination of buttermilk and apple-sauce

☞ Replaced traditional cream cheese frosting with a lower-fat one

Nutrition Scorecard *(per serving)*		
	Before	*After*
Calories	406	283
Fat (grams)	21	4
% calories from fat	46	12
Cholesterol (mg)	58	7

Carrot Spice Cake

1 cup whole-wheat flour

1 cup all-purpose flour

2 teaspoons baking soda

2½ teaspoons cinnamon

¾ teaspoon ground nutmeg

¾ teaspoon ground cloves

6 egg whites

1⅓ cups sugar

½ cup buttermilk

1 cup unsweetened applesauce

1 teaspoon vanilla extract

2 cups shredded peeled carrots

Cream Cheese Frosting

8 ounces tub-style light cream cheese

1 (7½-ounce) jar marshmallow creme

1 teaspoon fresh lemon juice

½ teaspoon vanilla extract

Preheat the oven to 350° F. Lightly coat a 13x9-inch baking pan with nonstick vegetable-oil spray.

To make the cake: In a large bowl, combine the whole-wheat flour, all-purpose flour, baking soda, cinnamon, nutmeg, and cloves. In another large bowl, beat the egg whites with an electric mixer on high speed until soft peaks form; gradually add the sugar. Gradually add the buttermilk, applesauce, and vanilla to the egg white mixture. Add the flour mixture. Fold in the carrots. Transfer the batter to the prepared baking pan.

Bake for 35 to 40 minutes, or until a toothpick inserted near the center comes out clean. Let the cake cool, in the pan, on a wire rack. Frost.

To make the frosting: In a medium bowl, combine the cream cheese, marshmallow creme, lemon juice, and vanilla. Take care not to overmix or frosting can become runny.

Hazelnut Torte Roll

Serves 10

❈❈❈❈❈

I especially enjoy making (and eating) jelly-roll style cakes. They're so attractive, and much easier to make than they appear. The hazelnuts add an incredible flavor.

How fat and calories were lowered:

🖝 Reduced the amount of nuts and added a bit of nugget cereal

🖝 Used egg whites in place of whole eggs

🖝 Reduced the amount of sugar

🖝 Created a fat-free filling rather than a buttercream filling

Nutrition Scorecard
(per serving)

	Before	After
Calories	623	181
Fat (grams)	38	6
% calories from fat	53	31
Cholesterol (mg)	129	3

Hazelnut Cake

¾ cup coarsely chopped hazelnuts, toasted

¼ cup nugget cereal (such as Grape-Nuts)

2 tablespoons all-purpose flour

8 egg whites

1 teaspoon cream of tartar

½ cup sugar

1 tablespoon powdered sugar

Cream Cheese–Ricotta Filling

½ cup fat-free cream cheese, at room temperature

½ cup powdered sugar

½ teaspoon vanilla extract

½ cup fat-free ricotta cheese

½ cup fat-free sour cream

Preheat the oven to 350° F. Lightly coat a 15x10x1-inch jelly-roll pan or baking sheet with nonstick vegetable-oil spray. Line the pan with wax paper, then spray the wax paper with nonstick spray.

To make the cake: In a food processor or blender, combine the toasted nuts, cereal, and flour. Blend until a crumblike texture is achieved; set aside.

In a large bowl, beat the egg whites and cream of tartar with an electric mixer on high speed (make sure the beaters are clean and dry) until soft peaks form (tips curl). Then slowly beat in the ½ cup sugar, beating until stiff peaks form (tips stand straight). Gently fold in about one-third of the nut mixture. Repeat, folding in remaining nut mixture by thirds. Spread the batter evenly in the prepared pan. (The 1 tablespoon powdered sugar will be used later.)

Bake 15 to 20 minutes, or until the cake springs back when lightly touched in the center. Meanwhile lightly sift the 1 tablespoon powdered sugar onto a clean dish towel.

Immediately loosen the cake from the sides of the pan and invert it onto the towel. Remove the wax paper and roll up the towel and the cake together, jelly-roll fashion, starting from a short end. Transfer the cake to a wire rack, seam side down, and let it cool completely.

To make the filling: In a small bowl, beat together the cream cheese, the ½ cup powdered sugar, and vanilla until well mixed. Fold in the ricotta and sour cream, one ingredient at a time.

To assemble the cake roll: Carefully unroll the cake. Spread the filling on the cake to within ½ inch of its edges. Carefully roll up the cake. Cover with plastic wrap and chill in the refrigerator for at least 1 hour. (Can be chilled overnight.)

Cinnamon Streusel Coffee Cake

Serves 12

❦❦ ❦❦ ❦❦

Wh) hen my neighbor tasted this, she proclaimed that she had found her new Christmas morning coffee cake. This cake uses streusel in the center and as a topping. It's my favorite coffee cake, too, with only half the calories and a fraction of the fat.

How fat and calories were lowered:

Cake:

☞ Used egg whites instead of whole eggs

☞ Reduced the amount of sugar

☞ Substituted applesauce for the butter

☞ Used fat-free sour cream

Streusel

☞ Reduced the amount of sugar

☞ Reduced the amount of nuts and added a little bit of oats in the topping

☞ Used light butter and significantly less of it

Nutrition Scorecard *(per serving)*		
	Before	*After*
Calories	629	306
Fat (grams)	39	6
% calories from fat	55	17
Cholesterol (mg)	159	1

Cinnamon Streusel

1 cup packed light brown sugar

1 tablespoon cinnamon

¾ cup chopped walnuts or pecans

1 tablespoon light butter, melted

2 tablespoons quick oats

Sour Cream Coffee Cake

1½ cups all-purpose flour

½ cup whole-wheat flour

1½ teaspoons baking powder

½ teaspoon baking soda

⅛ teaspoon salt

5 egg whites

1¼ cups sugar

½ cup unsweetened applesauce

1 cup fat-free sour cream (containing no gelatin)

2 teaspoons vanilla extract

To make the cinnamon streusel: In a small bowl, mix together the brown sugar and cinnamon. Add the nuts and stir. (The melted light butter and oats will be used later.)

To make the coffee cake: Preheat the oven to 350° F. Lightly coat a 9-inch round springform pan with nonstick vegetable-oil spray and set aside.

In a small bowl, combine the all-purpose flour, whole-wheat flour, baking powder, baking soda, and salt.

In a large bowl, beat the egg whites with an electric mixer on high setting until foamy. Gradually beat in the sugar until soft peaks form. Beat in the applesauce. Beat in the sour cream and vanilla. Add half the flour mixture and beat until blended. Add remaining flour mixture and beat until blended. Spoon half the batter into the prepared pan. Add half the streusel mixture (about 1 cup). Drop the remaining batter by spoonfuls over the streusel and carefully spread the batter evenly, using the back of a spoon. Add the melted light butter to the remaining streusel mixture and stir with a fork until blended. Sprinkle over the batter. Sprinkle the oats over the top. Bake 50 to 55 minutes, or until a toothpick inserted near the center of the cake comes out clean. Let cool, in pan, on wire rack. Serve warm or at room temperature.

Chocolate Orange Spice Cake

Serves 12

❧❧❧❧❧

With its satisfying combination of flavors, this is one of my favorite cakes.

How fat and calories were lowered:

For the glaze:

🖋 Used light butter and used less of it

🖋 Reduced the amount of sugar

For the cake:

🖋 Used fat-free sour cream

🖋 Replaced whole eggs with egg whites

🖋 Substituted baby-food prunes for vegetable oil

🖋 Replaced chocolate chips with mini chips and used less of them

<table>
<tr><td colspan="3">Nutrition Scorecard
(per serving)</td></tr>
<tr><td></td><td>Before</td><td>After</td></tr>
<tr><td>Calories</td><td>775</td><td>457</td></tr>
<tr><td>Fat (grams)</td><td>39</td><td>11</td></tr>
<tr><td>% calories from fat</td><td>49</td><td>23</td></tr>
<tr><td>Cholesterol (mg)</td><td>100</td><td>8</td></tr>
</table>

Glaze

¾ cup sugar

¼ cup light butter

¼ cup orange liqueur

3 tablespoons water

Cake:

8 egg whites

2 teaspoon instant coffee granules

1⅓ cup buttermilk

1 cup fat-free sour cream

2 (2½-ounce) jars baby-food prunes

2 tablespoons grated orange zest

1 teaspoon ground cinnamon

1 (18¼-ounce) box (2-layer) devil's food cake mix

1 (4-ounce) package instant chocolate fudge pudding mix

1 cup mini chocolate chips

1 tablespoon powdered sugar

To make the glaze: Combine the sugar, light butter, orange liqueur, and water in a heavy small saucepan. Stir over low heat until the butter melts and the sugar dissolves, about 3 minutes. Increase heat to medium-high and boil for 2 minutes. Cool completely.

To make the cake: Preheat the oven to 350° F. Lightly coat a 10-cup Bundt pan with nonstick vegetable-oil spray. In a large mixing bowl, using an electric mixer on high speed, beat the egg whites until foamy (about 30 seconds). Dissolve the instant coffee granules in the buttermilk. Add the buttermilk mixture, fat-free sour cream, baby-food prunes, zest, and cinnamon. Beat until blended. Add the cake mix and the pudding mix; beat for 3 minutes. Fold in the mini chocolate chips. (The 1 tablespoon powdered sugar will be used later.) Transfer the batter to the prepared Bundt pan and bake 55 to 60 minutes, or until a toothpick inserted near the center comes out with a few moist crumbs.

Immediately spoon the glaze mixture over the cake in the pan (it will run down the inside of the pan). Let stand 30 minutes. Turn the cake out onto a platter and cool. Sprinkle with the 1 tablespoon of powdered sugar and serve.

Mouthwatering

Cheesecakes

No-Bake Peanut Butter Cheese Pie

Serves 8

⋈ ⋈ ⋈ ⋈

This recipe was particularly challenging to make over, but the result was fabulous. I find that natural-style peanut butter has a richer, more peanutty taste.

How fat and calories were lowered:

🖝 Substituted pureed nonfat cottage cheese for the cream cheese

🖝 Used reduced-fat peanut butter, and less of it

🖝 Eliminated heavy cream and used a gelatin-milk combination

🖝 Used a combination of peanut butter and jam instead of butter in the crust

🖝 Reduced the amount of sugar

Nutrition Scorecard
(per serving)

	Before	After
Calories	703	392
Fat (grams)	53	11
% calories from fat	65	25
Cholesterol (mg)	79	1

Crust

2 tablespoons peach or apricot jam, melted

2 teaspoons peanut butter

1 cup graham cracker crumbs

Filling

⅓ cup nonfat milk

1 (¼-ounce) envelope unflavored gelatin

16 ounces nonfat cottage cheese

¾ cup reduced-fat natural-style chunky peanut butter

2½ cups powdered sugar

1 teaspoon vanilla extract

2 teaspoons fat-free fudge topping or fat-free chocolate syrup

To make the crust: Lightly coat an 8-inch springform pan with nonstick vegetable-oil spray. In a small bowl or cup, combine the melted jam and 2 teaspoons peanut butter. In another small bowl, combine graham crumbs and jam mixture with a fork. Press into the bottom of the prepared pan.

To make the filling: Put the nonfat milk in a small saucepan and sprinkle the gelatin over the top. Let stand 1 minute. On low heat, cook and stir until dissolved (do not boil). Remove from the heat and let cool to room temperature (about 10 minutes).

In a food processor or blender, puree the cottage cheese until smooth and creamy. Add ¾ cup peanut butter and pulse until smooth. Gradually add the powdered sugar and vanilla and pulse until smooth. Drizzle in the cooled gelatin mixture and blend until smooth. Pour into the prepared crust. Drizzle fat-free fudge over filling; use a toothpick or sharp knife to swirl in a decorative pattern. Chill until firm, about 2 hours.

How Much Sugar Is Okay?

The general rule of thumb is to keep sugar at 5–10 percent or less of your calories. This is because sugar itself offers no nutritional value except for calories. One gram of sugar has 4 calories. Roughly, this means 6 teaspoons (24 grams) of sugar for 1,600 calories; 12 teaspoons (48 grams) of sugar for 2,200 calories; and 18 teaspoons (72 grams) for 2,800.

Easy Mini Cheesecakes

Makes 24 mini cheesecakes

✂ ✂ ✂ ✂

$\mathcal{M}$y daughter gobbled these little gems up while requesting that they grace her lunch box. No problem!

How fat and calories were lowered:

☞ Used a combination of nonfat cottage cheese and light cream cheese instead of regular cream cheese

☞ Replaced regular milk with fat-free condensed milk

☞ Used egg whites instead of whole eggs

Nutrition Scorecard (per each mini cheesecake)		
	Before	After
Calories	219	114
Fat (grams)	15	3
% calories from fat	59	23
Cholesterol (mg)	68	8

24 ginger snap cookies (2-inch diameter)

1 cup nonfat cottage cheese

2 teaspoons vanilla extract

6 egg whites

8 ounces brick-style light cream cheese
   (not fat-free)

1 (14-ounce) can fat-free sweetened
   condensed milk

2 tablespoons all-purpose flour

Preheat the oven to 300° F. Lightly coat enough cupcake tins to make 24 cupcakes with nonstick vegetable-oil spray. Place one cookie in the bottom of each cup.

In a food processor or blender, puree the cottage cheese until smooth. Add the vanilla and egg whites and pulse until just blended. Add the light cream cheese, sweetened condensed milk, and flour, one ingredient at a time, pulsing until just blended after each addition.

Spoon about 3 tablespoons of the cream mixture into each tin. Bake 20 to 25 minutes, or until a knife inserted in the center comes out clean. Let cool on wire rack. Take a knife and loosen the rims of the mini cheesecakes. Remove them from the tins and chill, well covered.

Pumpkin Cheesecake

Serves 10

❈❈❈❈❈

Oh, this is sooo good. It took me five attempts to get this right and it was worth it. The key, I discovered, is knowing how and when you add the fat-free cream cheese. The fat-free cream cheese forms little lumps resembling cottage cheese when ingredients other than sugar are added to it. But I found that softening the fat-free cream cheese at room temperature and then beating it with the light cream cheese first, then mixing in the sugar after that took care of this problem. So do be careful when following these directions; otherwise you may end up with a lumpy (although still delicious) cheesecake.

Nutrition Scorecard *(per serving)*		
	Before	After
Calories	516	257
Fat (grams)	35	5
% calories from fat	60	18
Cholesterol (mg)	184	13

How fat and calories were lowered:

☛ Used jam instead of butter to bind the cookie crust

☛ Replaced regular cream cheese with a combination of fat-free cream cheese, light cream cheese, and pureed nonfat cottage cheese

☛ Replaced whole eggs with egg whites

Ginger Snap Crust

15 ginger snaps

2 tablespoons apricot or peach jam, melted

Pumpkin Cheesecake Filling

8 ounces fat-free cream cheese, at room
temperature

8 ounces tub-style light cream cheese
(not fat-free), at room temperature

1¼ cups sugar

1 cup nonfat cottage cheese

1⅓ cups canned pumpkin (not pie filling)

1 tablespoon vanilla extract

1½ teaspoons cinnamon

1 teaspoon all-purpose flour

¼ teaspoon ground allspice

¼ teaspoon ground cloves

6 egg whites

Preheat the oven to 325° F. Lightly coat an 8- or 9-inch springform pan with nonstick vegetable-oil spray.

To make the crust: In a food processor or blender, grind the ginger snaps until crumbly. In a large bowl, combine the ginger snap crumbs and melted jam with a fork. Mix until blended and press into the bottom of the prepared pan.

To make the filling: In a large bowl, beat together the fat-free cream cheese and light cream cheese with an electric mixer on the lowest speed until blended. Beat in the sugar.

In a food processor or blender, puree the cottage cheese until smooth and creamy. Add the pumpkin, vanilla, cinnamon, flour, allspice, and cloves. Blend until smooth. Add the pumpkin mixture to the cream cheese mixture and mix just until blended. Add the egg whites and mix just until blended. Pour the mixture into the prepared pan.

Bake 80 minutes, or until the cheesecake puffs and the center is almost set. Transfer to a wire rack and let cool. To serve, run a knife around the sides to loosen the cake. Release the pan sides. Cut into wedges.

Light Cream Cheese: Packaging Counts

You would have to be a food-label sleuth to notice that light cream cheese packaged in the brick style has 1 more gram of fat per serving than the tub version. That's an extra 8 grams per package. That's why in all my recipes calling for light cream cheese, I specify the tub version!

✄ ✄ ✄ ✄ ✄

Peachy Cheesecake

Serves 12

⚜️⚜️⚜️⚜️⚜️

This nearly fat-free cheesecake is creamy and irresistible. How fat and calories were lowered:

- Replaced whole eggs with egg whites
- Used fat-free cream cheese instead of regular cream cheese
- Used fat-free sour cream instead of regular sour cream
- Eliminated the butter in the crust

Nutrition Scorecard *(per serving)*		
	Before	After
Calories	520	226
Fat (grams)	32	0.5
% calories from fat	54	2
Cholesterol (mg)	106	10

½ cup graham cracker crumbs

Cheesecake

24 ounces fat-free cream cheese, at room temperature

¾ cup sugar

2 teaspoons vanilla extract

6 egg whites

Sour Cream Peach Topping

1 cup fat-free sour cream (containing no gelatin)

1 (21-ounce) can peach pie filling

1 recipe Peach Glaze (page 57)

Preheat the oven to 325° F. Lightly coat a 9-inch springform pan with nonstick vegetable-oil spray. Sprinkle the graham crumbs evenly over bottom of pan.

To make the cheesecake: In a large bowl, beat together the cream cheese, sugar, and vanilla with an electric mixer on the lowest setting, until blended. Add the egg whites and mix until blended (take care not to overbeat). Pour the filling over the crumbs in the pan.

Bake 45 minutes, or until cheesecake puffs and the center is almost set. Remove from oven and prepare the sour cream topping. (Do not turn off oven.)

To make the topping: Mix together the fat-free sour cream and pie filling. Spread over the cheesecake and return it to the oven for 10 minutes. Let cool, in the pan, on a wire rack. Top with the peach glaze. Chill.

To serve, run a knife around the sides to loosen the cake. Release the pan sides. Cut the cheesecake into wedges.

Almost Fat-Free Cheesecake

Serves 12

❊❊❊❊❊

I was surprised at how good this cheesecake tastes with almost no fat. The sour cream layer gives it a creamy texture. You'll be proud to serve it to guests, but shh, don't tell them it's low in fat—they'll never know.

How fat and calories were lowered:

☞ Eliminated the butter in the crust

☞ Used fat-free cream cheese

☞ Replaced the whole eggs with egg whites

☞ Used fat-free sour cream in the topping instead of regular sour cream

Nutrition Scorecard (per serving)		
	Before	After
Calories	552	182
Fat (grams)	40	0.5
% calories from fat	64	3
Cholesterol (mg)	170	10

½ cup graham cracker crumbs

Filling

24 ounces fat-free cream cheese, at room temperature

1 cup sugar

1 teaspoon vanilla extract

6 egg whites

Sour Cream Topping

16 ounces fat-free sour cream (containing no gelatin)

3 tablespoons sugar

1 teaspoon vanilla extract

Preheat the oven to 325° F. Lightly coat a 9-inch springform pan with nonstick vegetable-oil spray. Sprinkle graham crumbs evenly over the bottom of the pan.

To make the filling: In a large bowl, beat together the cream cheese, sugar, and vanilla with an electric mixer on the lowest setting until blended. Add the egg whites and mix until blended (take care not to overbeat). Pour filling over crumbs in pan.

Bake 45 minutes, or until cheesecake puffs and the center is almost set. Remove from oven and prepare sour cream topping. (Do not turn off oven.)

To make the sour cream topping: In a small bowl, combine the fat-free sour cream, sugar, and vanilla. Spread over the hot cheesecake. Return to the oven for 5 to 7 minutes, or until the topping is set.

Transfer the cheesecake to a rack and let cool. Cover and chill at least 1 hour. To serve, run a knife around the sides to loosen the cake. Release the pan sides. Cut the cheesecake into wedges.

How to End a Chocolate Craving

Eat it! Researchers at the University of Pennsylvania found that when women were given substitutes for chocolate, their craving persisted. But when they ate a *real* chocolate bar, the craving disappeared. Chocolate cravings are the most common cravings in North America!

Source: M.W. Rozin, *Physiology and Behavior* 56 (3): 419-22 (1994).

Almond Amaretto Cheesecake

Serves 12

❧❧❧❧❧

This is one of the best cheesecakes I've tasted. You do need to plan ahead a bit to make the vanilla yogurt cheese—which is a snap to do. If you are pressed for time, however, you can substitute one cup pureed nonfat cottage cheese. Be sure to toast the almonds to bring out the rich nutty flavor.

How fat and calories were lowered:

Crust:

☞ Used reduced-fat vanilla wafers

☞ Eliminated the butter

Nutrition Scorecard		
(per serving)		
	Before	*After*
Calories	441	236
Fat (grams)	32	6
% calories from fat	67	24
Cholesterol (mg)	150	14

Filling:

☞ Used a combination of yogurt cheese, light cream cheese, and fat-free cream cheese in place of regular cream cheese

☞ Eliminated the cream

☞ Used egg whites in place of the whole eggs

☞ Reduced the amount of almonds

☞ Reduced the amount of chocolate chips

Vanilla Yogurt Cheese

2 cups nonfat vanilla yogurt

Vanilla Wafer Almond Crust

12 reduced-fat vanilla wafer cookies

3 tablespoons chopped toasted almonds

Amaretto Filling

16 ounces fat-free cream cheese, at room temperature

8 ounces tub-style light cream cheese, at room temperature

¾ cup sugar

2 tablespoons all-purpose flour

½ cup amaretto

2 teaspoons almond extract

6 egg whites

3 tablespoons chopped toasted almonds

4 teaspoons chocolate chips, melted

To make the yogurt cheese: Line a strainer with a double layer of cheesecloth or a coffee filter. Place the strainer over a deep bowl to allow the whey to drip off. Put the yogurt into the lined strainer and let it drain in the refrigerator overnight, or until thickened (at least 4 hours).

To make the crust: Lightly coat a 9-inch springform pan with nonstick vegetable-oil spray. In a food processor or blender, grind the cookies into coarse crumbs. Add the 3 tablespoons toasted almonds and pulse until blended. Sprinkle the crumb mixture evenly onto the bottom of the prepared pan.

To make the filling: In a large bowl, beat together the fat-free cream cheese and light cream cheese with an electric mixer on the lowest speed until blended. Gradually beat in the sugar and flour. Add the vanilla yogurt cheese and mix until smooth. Beat in the amaretto and almond extract. Add the egg whites and beat just until smooth. Stir in the 3 tablespoons toasted almonds. Pour the filling over the crumbs in the pan.

Preheat oven to 325° F. Bake the cheesecake for 70 to 75 minutes, or until it puffs and the center is almost set. Transfer to a rack and let cool. To serve, run a knife around the sides to loosen the cake. Release the pan sides. Drizzle melted chocolate chips over the cheesecake.

Lime Daiquiri Cheesecake

Serves 12

✄ ✄ ✄ ✄ ✄

Lime lovers plead for the recipe for this cheesecake, which tastes remarkably like the drink that it's fashioned after.

How fat and calories were lowered:

☞ Used a plain graham cracker crumb crust

☞ Replaced regular cream cheese with a combination of fat-free cream cheese, light cream cheese, and pureed cottage cheese

☞ Used egg whites in place of whole eggs

Nutrition Scorecard
(per serving)

	Before	After
Calories	445	247
Fat (grams)	27	4
% calories from fat	55	11
Cholesterol (mg)	161	14

½ cup graham cracker crumbs

Filling

16 ounces fat-free cream cheese, at room temperature

8 ounces tub-style light cream cheese (not fat-free)

1 cup sugar

2 tablespoons flour

1 cup nonfat cottage cheese

½ cup frozen limeade concentrate, thawed

3 tablespoons fresh lime juice

1½ teaspoons imitation rum extract

1 teaspoon finely grated lime zest

6 egg whites

Lime Glaze

3 tablespoons sugar

1 tablespoon cornstarch

½ cup frozen limeade concentrate, thawed

1 teaspoon imitation rum extract

2 teaspoons fresh lime juice

1 teaspoon finely grated lime zest

Preheat the oven to 325° F. Lightly coat a 9-inch springform pan with nonstick vegetable-oil spray. Sprinkle graham cracker crumbs evenly over the bottom of the pan.

To make the filling: In a large bowl, beat together the fat-free cream cheese and light cream cheese with an electric mixer on the lowest speed until blended. Gradually beat in the 1 cup sugar and the flour. In a food processor or blender, puree the cottage cheese until it is smooth and resembles fluffy marshmallow creme. Add the pureed cottage cheese to the cream cheese mixture and mix until smooth. Beat in the ½ cup limeade concentrate, the 3 tablespoons lime juice, 1½ teaspoons rum extract, and the 1 teaspoon lime zest. Add the egg whites and beat just until smooth. Pour the filling over the crumbs in the pan.

Bake at 325° F. for 70 to 75 minutes, or until the cheesecake puffs and the center is almost set. Transfer to a wire rack and let cool. Run a knife around the sides to loosen the cake. Release the pan sides. Chill, uncovered, overnight. Top with the glaze.

To make the glaze: In small saucepan, combine the 3 tablespoons sugar and the cornstarch. Add the ½ cup limeade concentrate, the 1 teaspoon rum extract, and the 2 teaspoons lime juice. Cook and stir over medium heat until bubbly. Cook and stir 2 minutes more. Remove from heat. Stir in the 1 teaspoon lime zest. Pour the glaze over the cheesecake. Chill until serving time.

Piña Colada Cheesecake

Serves 12

❧❧❧❧❧

A tropical delight that's sure to please.
How fat and calories were lowered:

☛ Reduced the amount of coconut

☛ Used egg whites instead of whole eggs

☛ Used coconut extract instead of cream of coconut

☛ Used a combination of fat-free cream cheese, light cream cheese, and pureed cottage cheese instead of regular cream cheese

Nutrition Scorecard
(per serving)

	Before	After
Calories	447	211
Fat (grams)	32	5
% calories from fat	63	23
Cholesterol (mg)	141	11

Crust

⅓ cup graham cracker crumbs

¼ cup flaked coconut

Filling

8 ounces fat-free cream cheese

8 ounces tub-style light cream cheese
(not fat-free)

¾ cup sugar

2 tablespoons flour

1 cup nonfat cottage cheese

½ cup frozen pineapple juice concentrate,
thawed

1½ teaspoons coconut extract

1 (8-ounce) can crushed pineapple
(juice-packed), well drained

¼ cup flaked coconut

6 egg whites

Pineapple Glaze

1 tablespoon sugar

1 tablespoon cornstarch

½ cup frozen pineapple juice concentrate,
thawed

2 tablespoons flaked coconut

Preheat the oven to 325° F. Lightly coat a 9-inch springform pan with nonstick vegetable-oil spray. Sprinkle the graham cracker crumbs and ¼ cup coconut evenly over the bottom of the pan.

To make the filling: In a large bowl, beat together the fat-free cream cheese and light cream cheese with an electric mixer on the lowest speed until blended. Gradually beat in the ¾ cup sugar and the flour. In a food processor or blender, puree the cottage cheese until it is smooth and resembles fluffy marshmallow creme. Add the pureed cottage cheese to the cream cheese mixture and mix until smooth. Beat in the pineapple juice concentrate and coconut extract. Add the crushed pineapple and ¼ cup coconut and beat until blended. Add the egg whites and beat just until smooth. Pour the filling over the crumbs and coconut in the pan.

Bake for 70 to 75 minutes, or until the cheesecake puffs and the center is almost set. Transfer to a rack. Let cool for 15 minutes, then run a knife around the sides to loosen the cake. Release the pan sides. Chill, uncovered, overnight. Top with the glaze.

To make the glaze: In a small saucepan, combine the 1 tablespoon sugar and the cornstarch. Add the ½ cup pineapple juice concentrate and cook and stir over medium heat until bubbly. Cook and stir 1 minute more. Remove from the heat and pour over the cheesecake. Sprinkle the 2 tablespoons coconut over the glaze. Chill until serving time.

Very Blueberry Swirl Cheesecake

Serves 12

⊰⊱ ⊰⊱ ⊰⊱ ⊰⊱

This cheesecake is crowned with an intense blueberry topping that's baked into the cheesecake. Fresh or frozen blueberries work well.

How fat and calories were lowered:

🖙 Used a plain graham cracker crust only on the bottom

🖙 Replaced regular cream cheese with a combination of fat-free cream cheese, light cream cheese, and pureed cottage cheese

🖙 Used egg whites instead of whole eggs

🖙 Used fat-free sour cream

Nutrition Scorecard (per serving)		
	Before	After
Calories	429	209
Fat (grams)	28	4
% calories from fat	59	17
Cholesterol (mg)	146	11

½ cup graham cracker crumbs

Blueberry Puree

1½ cups fresh or frozen blueberries

¼ cup sugar

2 teaspoons cornstarch

1 tablespoon fresh lemon juice

Cheesecake

8 ounces fat-free cream cheese

8 ounces tub-style light cream cheese (not fat-free)

1 cup sugar

2 tablespoons flour

1 cup nonfat cottage cheese

2 teaspoons vanilla extract

1 cup fat-free sour cream (containing no gelatin)

6 egg whites

Preheat the oven to 350° F. Tightly cover the outside bottom and sides of a 9-inch springform pan with heavy-duty foil (to make it waterproof). Lightly coat the inside of the pan with nonstick vegetable-oil spray. Sprinkle the graham crumbs evenly over the bottom of the pan.

To make the blueberry puree: Combine the blueberries, the ¼ cup sugar, and the cornstarch in a medium saucepan. Bring to a boil over medium heat (with the sugar and heat, the blueberries will become liquidy); cook, stirring, an additional 5 minutes. Puree the mixture in a blender or food processor with the lemon juice. Let cool completely.

To make the cheesecake: In a large bowl, beat together the fat-free cream cheese and light cream cheese with an electric mixer on the lowest speed until blended. Gradually beat in the 1 cup sugar and the flour. In a food processor or blender, puree the cottage cheese until it is smooth and resembles fluffy marshmallow creme. Add the pureed cottage cheese to the cream cheese mixture and mix until smooth. Beat in the vanilla extract and fat-free sour cream. Add the egg whites and beat just until smooth.

Pour the filling over the crumbs in the pan and set the pan in a large roasting pan. Carefully drizzle the blueberry puree over the batter. Swirl a thin knife through the batter to marbleize it. Place the pan on the oven rack. Carefully pour enough boiling water into the roasting pan to come 1 inch up the sides of the springform pan. Bake 75 minutes, or until the center is set. Turn oven off; let the cheesecake stand in the oven 1 hour.

Remove the cheesecake pan from the water bath. Let cool completely on a wire rack. Remove the foil. Cover and refrigerate overnight. Just before serving, run a knife around the edges of the pan and remove sides.

Mint Chocolate Marble Cheesecake

Serves 12

❈ ❈ ❈ ❈ ❈

Ribbons of chocolate cheesecake are swirled into a minty green cheesecake for a show-stopping dessert that could double as a table centerpiece. How fat and calories were lowered:

🖝 Used a plain chocolate cookie crumb crust without butter

🖝 Replaced the regular cream cheese with a combination of fat-free cream cheese, light cream cheese, and pureed cottage cheese

🖝 Eliminated the sour cream

🖝 Replaced the whole eggs with egg whites

Nutrition Scorecard (per serving)		
	Before	After
Calories	382	220
Fat (grams)	26	5
% calories from fat	62	22
Cholesterol (mg)	144	14

10 chocolate wafer cookies (2½-inch diameter), crushed

Filling

8 ounces fat-free cream cheese

8 ounces tub-style light cream cheese (not fat-free)

¾ cup sugar

2 tablespoons flour

1 cup nonfat cottage cheese

6 egg whites

2 tablespoons unsweetened cocoa powder

3 tablespoons sugar

½ cup crème de menthe

1 teaspoon peppermint extract

Preheat the oven to 325° F. Lightly coat a 9-inch springform pan with nonstick vegetable-oil spray. Sprinkle the cookie crumbs evenly over the bottom of the pan.

To make the filling: In a large bowl, beat together the fat-free cream cheese and light cream cheese with an electric mixer on the lowest speed until blended. Gradually beat in the ¾ cup sugar and the flour. In a food processor or blender, puree the cottage cheese until it is smooth and resembles fluffy marshmallow creme. Add the pureed cottage cheese to the cream cheese mixture and mix until smooth. Add the egg whites and beat just until smooth.

Remove ¾ cup of the mixture and put into a small bowl; stir in the cocoa powder and the 3 tablespoons sugar.

Stir crème de menthe and peppermint extract into the remaining plain cream cheese mixture.

Pour half of the crème de menthe mixture over the crust. Spoon two-thirds of the chocolate mixture over the crème de menthe mixture. Pour the remaining crème de menthe mixture over the chocolate mixture. Top with the remaining chocolate mixture. Without disturbing the crust, swirl the blade of a knife through the cake to create a marbling effect.

Bake for 65 to 70 minutes, or until the cheesecake puffs and the center is almost set. Transfer to a rack and let cool completely, then run a knife around the sides to loosen the cake. Release the pan sides. Cover and chill overnight.

Cranberry Orange Cheesecake

Serves 12

✄ ✄ ✄ ✄ ✄

Cranberries may scream "Thanksgiving," but this cheesecake is so wonderful you'll want to serve it year-round. Be sure to buy extra bags of fresh cranberries during the fall and freeze a few for a seasonless treat.

How fat and calories were lowered:

☞ Used a plain graham cracker crust

☞ Replaced regular cream cheese with a combination of fat-free cream cheese, light cream cheese, and pureed cottage cheese

☞ Used egg whites instead of whole eggs

☞ Reduced the amount of walnuts

☞ Reduced the amount of cranberry juice concentrate

Nutrition Scorecard
(per serving)

	Before	After
Calories	520	211
Fat (grams)	31	5
% calories from fat	52	23
Cholesterol (mg)	133	11

½ cup graham cracker crumbs

Cranberry Orange Cheesecake

8 ounces fat-free cream cheese

8 ounces tub-style light cream cheese (not fat-free)

¾ cup sugar

2 tablespoons flour

1 cup nonfat cottage cheese

⅓ cup frozen cranberry juice cocktail concentrate, thawed

2 teaspoons finely grated orange zest

1 teaspoon vanilla extract

1 cup fresh cranberries, finely chopped

¼ cup finely chopped walnuts

6 egg whites

Orange Sour Cream Topping

1 cup fat-free sour cream

2 tablespoons sugar

1½ teaspoons finely grated orange zest

Preheat the oven to 325° F. Lightly coat a 9-inch springform pan with nonstick vegetable-oil spray. Sprinkle the graham cracker crumbs evenly on the bottom of pan.

To make the cheesecake: In a large bowl, beat together the fat-free cream cheese and light cream cheese with an electric mixer on the lowest speed until blended. Gradually beat in the ¾ cup sugar and the flour. In a food processor or blender, puree the cottage cheese until it is smooth and resembles fluffy marshmallow creme. Add the pureed cottage cheese to the cream cheese mixture and mix until smooth. Gradually beat in the cranberry juice concentrate, the 2 teaspoons orange zest, and the vanilla. Add the chopped cranberries and walnuts and beat until blended. Add the egg whites and beat just until smooth. Pour the filling over the crumbs in the pan.

Bake for 60 to 65 minutes, or until the cheesecake puffs and the center is almost set. Transfer to a wire rack. Let cool completely, then run a knife around the sides to loosen the cake. Release the pan sides. Cover and chill, overnight. Cover with the topping.

To make the topping: In a small bowl, stir together the fat-free sour cream, the 2 tablespoons sugar, and the 1½ teaspoons orange zest. Spread over the chilled cheesecake. Chill until serving time.

Lemon Cheesecake

Serves 12

❈❈❈❈❈

Pucker up for this one—it's fantastic.

How fat and calories were lowered:

🖙 Used a plain graham cracker crust

🖙 Replaced regular cream cheese with a combination of fat-free cream cheese, light cream cheese, and pureed cottage cheese

🖙 Used mostly egg whites instead of whole eggs. (Retained one whole egg for added lemon color.)

🖙 Used fat-free sour cream

Nutrition Scorecard		
(per serving)		
	Before	*After*
Calories	451	207
Fat (grams)	32	4
% calories from fat	62	19
Cholesterol (mg)	154	28

Crust

½ cup graham cracker crumbs

1 teaspoon finely grated lemon zest

Lemon Cheesecake

8 ounces fat-free cream cheese

8 ounces tub-style light cream cheese

¾ cup sugar

2 tablespoons flour

1 cup nonfat cottage cheese

¼ cup fat-free sour cream (containing no gelatin)

½ cup frozen lemonade concentrate, thawed

2 tablespoons fresh lemon juice

1 tablespoon finely grated lemon zest

2 teaspoons vanilla extract

4 egg whites

1 whole egg

Lemon Sour Cream Topping

1 cup fat-free sour cream

3 tablespoons sugar

2 teaspoons finely grated lemon zest

Lemon slices, for garnish

Preheat the oven to 325° F. Lightly coat a 9-inch springform pan with nonstick vegetable-oil spray. Mix together the graham cracker crumbs and lemon zest, then sprinkle evenly on the bottom of the pan.

To make the cheesecake: In a large bowl, beat together the fat-free cream cheese and light cream cheese with an electric mixer on the lowest speed until blended. Gradually beat in the ¾ cup sugar and the flour. In a food processor or blender, puree the cottage cheese until it is smooth and resembles fluffy marshmallow creme. Add the pureed cottage cheese to the cream cheese mixture and mix until smooth. Beat in the ¼ cup fat-free sour cream. Gradually beat in the lemonade concentrate, fresh lemon juice, 1 tablespoon lemon zest, and vanilla. Add the egg whites and whole egg and beat just until smooth. Pour the filling over the crust in the pan.

Bake for 60 to 65 minutes, or until the cheesecake puffs and the center is almost set. Transfer to a wire rack. Let cool completely, then run a knife around the sides to loosen the cake. Release the pan sides. Cover and chill, overnight. Add the topping.

To make the topping: In a small bowl, stir together the 1 cup fat-free sour cream, the 3 tablespoons sugar, and the 2 teaspoons lemon zest. Spread over the chilled cheese-cake. Garnish with the lemon slices and chill until serving time.

Pecan Caramel Cheesecake

Serves 12

❈ ❈ ❈ ❈ ❈

Toasted pecan bits with a splash of bourbon take center stage in this New Orleans–style cheesecake. A fat-free caramel topping is drizzled over the cheesecake for a little extra mouthwatering appeal.

How fat and calories were lowered:

🖘 Used a plain vanilla wafer crumb crust

🖘 Replaced regular cream cheese with a combination of fat-free cream cheese, light cream cheese, and pureed cottage cheese

🖘 Used egg whites instead of whole eggs

🖘 Reduced the amount of pecans

Nutrition Scorecard *(per serving)*		
	Before	After
Calories	507	247
Fat (grams)	38	8
% calories from fat	67	33
Cholesterol (mg)	179	14

12 reduced-fat vanilla wafer cookies, crushed

Filling

8 ounces fat-free cream cheese

8 ounces tub-style light cream cheese (not fat-free)

½ cup white sugar

½ cup packed dark brown sugar

2 tablespoons flour

1 cup nonfat cottage cheese

3 tablespoons bourbon

6 egg whites

⅔ cup chopped toasted pecans

¼ cup fat-free caramel topping

Preheat the oven to 325° F. Lightly coat a 9-inch springform pan with nonstick vegetable-oil spray. Sprinkle cookie crumbs evenly over bottom of pan.

In a large bowl, beat together the fat-free cream cheese and light cream cheese with an electric mixer on the lowest speed until blended. Beat in the white sugar. Add the brown sugar and flour and beat until blended. In a food processor or blender, puree the cottage cheese until it is smooth and resembles fluffy marshmallow creme. Add the pureed cottage cheese to the cream cheese mixture and mix until smooth. Gradually beat in the bourbon. Add the egg whites and beat just until smooth. Stir in the pecans. Bake for 65 to 70 minutes, or until the cheesecake puffs and the center is almost set. Transfer to a wire rack. Let cool completely, then run a knife around the sides to loosen the cake. Release the pan sides. Cover and chill, overnight. Drizzle with the fat-free caramel topping.

Mint Chocolate Marble Cheesecake

Very Blueberry Swirl Cheesecake

Triple Chocolate Cheesecake

Chocolate Crunch Ice Cream Balls

Triple Chocolate Cheesecake

Serves 12

❄❄ ❄❄ ❄❄

A *glorious chocolaty treat accented by white chocolate.*
How fat and calories were lowered:

☞ Used a plain chocolate cookie crust

☞ Replaced regular cream cheese with a combination of fat-free cream cheese, light cream cheese, and pureed cottage cheese

☞ Used egg whites instead of whole eggs

☞ Reduced the amount of chocolate chips and partially replaced them with cocoa powder

☞ Reduced the amount of white chocolate topping

Nutrition Scorecard
(per serving)

	Before	After
Calories	722	225
Fat (grams)	55	8
% calories from fat	65	32
Cholesterol (mg)	162	12

Chocolate Cheesecake

10 chocolate wafer cookies (2½-inch diameter), crushed

8 ounces fat-free cream cheese

8 ounces tub-style light cream cheese (not fat-free)

1 cup sugar

¼ cup unsweetened cocoa powder

2 tablespoons flour

1 cup nonfat cottage cheese

2 teaspoons almond extract

½ cup chocolate chips, melted

6 egg whites

White Chocolate Glaze

1 ounce white chocolate, melted

Preheat the oven to 325° F. Lightly coat a 9-inch springform pan with nonstick vegetable-oil spray. Sprinkle the cookie crumbs evenly over bottom of the pan.

In a large bowl, beat together the fat-free cream cheese and light cream cheese with an electric mixer on the lowest speed until blended. In a small bowl, combine the sugar, cocoa powder, and flour. Add the sugar mixture to the cream cheese mixture and mix until smooth. In a food processor or blender, puree the cottage cheese until it is smooth and resembles fluffy marshmallow creme. Add the pureed cottage cheese and almond extract to the cream cheese mixture and mix until smooth. While beating, drizzle in the melted chocolate chips and mix until smooth. Add the egg whites and beat just until smooth. Bake for 65 to 70 minutes, or until the cheesecake puffs and the center is almost set. Transfer to a wire rack. Let cool completely, then run a knife around the sides to loosen the cake and release pan sides. Cover and chill, overnight.

Drizzle the melted white chocolate over the cheesecake. Chill until serving time.

Raspberry Cheesecake

Serves 10

❧❧❧❧❧

Any fresh berry (strawberry, blackberry) makes a wonderful finishing crown. Just be sure to use either a neutral tasting jam such as apricot, or a jam that matches your berry's flavor.

How fat and calories were lowered:

☞ Replaced regular cream cheese with a combination of vanilla yogurt cheese, nonfat cottage cheese, and light cream cheese

☞ Used egg whites in place of whole eggs

☞ Reduced the almonds and made up the difference with extra cookie crumbs. The toasted almonds add a flavorful texture to the crust.

Nutrition Scorecard *(per serving)*		
	Before	After
Calories	523	197
Fat (grams)	39	5
% calories from fat	67	24
Cholesterol (mg)	136	8

Yogurt Cheese

2 cups nonfat vanilla yogurt

Vanilla Wafer Almond Crust

3 tablespoons whole almonds
12 reduced-fat vanilla wafers

Filling

1 cup nonfat cottage cheese
8 ounces tub-style light cream cheese
     (not fat-free)

¾ cup sugar
1 tablespoon all-purpose flour
1 teaspoon finely grated lemon
4 egg whites

Topping

1 pint raspberries
½ cup seedless raspberry jam

To make the yogurt cheese: Line a strainer with a double layer of cheesecloth or a coffee filter. Place the strainer over a deep bowl to allow the whey to drip off. Put the yogurt into a lined strainer and let it drain in the refrigerator overnight until thickened.

Place the almonds under the broiler and toast until light brown and aromatic (about 3 to 5 minutes). In a food processor or blender, combine the vanilla wafers and toasted almonds; pulse until they are fine crumbs. Spray a 9-inch springform pan with nonstick vegetable-oil spray. Lightly press the crumbs onto the bottom of the springform pan.

Preheat the oven to 350° F.

To make the filling: In a food processor or blender, puree the cottage cheese until creamy. Add the yogurt cheese, light cream cheese, sugar, flour, and lemon zest and puree until smooth. Add the egg whites and puree until smooth. (Take care not to overblend the filling, to prevent cracking during baking.)

Pour the filling mixture on top of the crumbs. Bake for 50 minutes, or until the cheesecake puffs and the center is almost set. Let cool 15 minutes on a wire rack. Loosen the cheesecake from sides of pan. Let cool 30 minutes more; remove the sides of the pan. Add the raspberry topping. Chill at least 3 hours.

To make the raspberry topping: Cover the cheesecake with the raspberries. Melt the raspberry jam (about 45 seconds on High in the microwave). With a pastry brush, gently brush the jam over the berries.

Fiber-Rich Raspberries

One cup of raspberries has nearly 8 grams of fiber (more than twice the fiber of a bowl of oatmeal). That's one reason I'm fond of leaving the seeds in raspberry sauces (to the chagrin of some of my culinary pals)—raspberries are high in fiber because of their seed content. I also enjoy the texture they offer in a sauce or compote. So save yourself a step and keep the seeds in if you wish.

❄ ❄ ❄ ❄ ❄

Strawberry Surprise Cheesecake

Serves 8

✄ ✄ ✄ ✄ ✄

I *was asked to make an enticing recipe using tofu for a television show. Since there's nothing like using a dessert to lure someone into tasting a novel ingredient, I came up with this cheesecake. It was a hit, enjoyed by one and all. In fact, my daughter, who ardently claims to dislike tofu, tasted this pie and proceeded to eat two servings. I still haven't told her that she's been eating tofu.*

How fat and calories were lowered:

☛ Replaced part of the cream cheese with light tofu

☛ Used light cream cheese instead of regular cream cheese

☛ Used egg whites instead of whole eggs

☛ Used a ready-made reduced-fat graham cracker crust

☛ Used low-sugar preserves for an easy glaze

Nutrition Scorecard		
(per serving)		
	Before	*After*
Calories	397	255
Fat (grams)	25	9
% calories from fat	57	30
Cholesterol (mg)	62	10

1 (10.5 ounce) package light extra-firm tofu

1 (8-ounce) tub-style light cream cheese (not fat-free), softened at room temperature

½ cup sugar

1 teaspoon finely shredded lemon zest

½ teaspoon vanilla extract

3 egg whites

1 ready-made reduced-fat graham cracker crust

10 ounces (2 cups) strawberries, washed, hulled, and sliced in half, lengthwise

¼ cup low-sugar strawberry preserves

Preheat the oven to 350° F. In a food processor or blender, puree the tofu until smooth and creamy. In a large mixing bowl, using an electric mixer, beat the cream cheese and sugar until smooth. Add the pureed tofu, lemon zest, and vanilla and mix until smooth. Add the egg whites and mix until just blended. Pour into the graham cracker crust. Bake for 45 to 50 minutes, or until firm. Remove from the oven and cool to room temperature.

Arrange the strawberries decoratively (cut-side down) on top of the cheesecake. Microwave the preserves until melted (about 15 seconds). Drizzle over the strawberries. Chill at least 2 hours.

No-Hassle,

No-Fuss,

In-a-Pinch

Desserts

Boston Cream Pie

Serves 6

It's hard to believe that a dessert that looks and taste so good is a cinch to make, but it is, thanks to a head start with a commercial loaf cake. How fat and calories were lowered:

☞ Used nonfat milk instead of whole milk

☞ Reduced the amount of chocolate chips

☞ Used a fat-free loaf cake

Nutrition Scorecard
(per serving)

	Before	After
Calories	342	290
Fat (grams)	16	3
% calories from fat	39	11
Cholesterol (mg)	117	0

1 (3.4-ounce) package instant vanilla pudding

1 cup nonfat milk

1 teaspoon imitation rum extract

⅓ cup semisweet chocolate chips

1 (14-ounce) loaf fat-free golden cake

In a medium bowl, whisk together the pudding mix, milk, and rum extract for 1 to 2 minutes, until thickened. Let stand while preparing the cake.

In a glass measure or dish, combine the chocolate chips and 1 tablespoon water. Microwave on High for 35 to 45 seconds, or until the chocolate is melted and smooth when stirred.

Slice the loaf cake horizontally into 3 equal layers. Place the bottom layer on a serving plate. Spread half the pudding mixture evenly over the cake. Cover with the middle cake layer. Spread evenly with the remaining pudding mixture and top with the remaining cake layer, cut side down.

Spread the melted chocolate evenly over the top. Serve immediately or refrigerate. Cut into slices with a large serrated knife.

Amaretto Chocolate Pudding

Serves 4

✄ ✄ ✄ ✄ ✄

This rich chocolate dessert is easy to make, with its base of chocolate pudding mix.

How fat and calories were lowered:

☞ Reduced the amount of chocolate chips

☞ Used nonfat milk instead of whole milk

☞ Reduced the amount of liqueur

☞ Eliminated the whipped topping

Nutrition Scorecard
(per serving)

	Before	After
Calories	439	206
Fat (grams)	20	3
% calories from fat	43	14
Cholesterol (mg)	54	2

1 (3.4-ounce) package cook-and-serve chocolate pudding mix (not instant)

1½ cups nonfat milk

3 tablespoons amaretto or 1 teaspoon almond extract

3 tablespoons semisweet chocolate chips

Pour the pudding mix into a heavy medium saucepan. Gradually stir in the milk and amaretto. Cook and stir over medium heat until the pudding comes to a boil and thickens. Add the chocolate chips and stir until melted and thoroughly blended. Pour into 4 dessert glasses. Cover and chill.

Chocolate Crunch Ice Cream Balls

Serves 4

❧❧❧❧❧

Kids will love to help make these treats.
How fat and calories were lowered:

- Reduced the amount of chocolate chips and nuts
- Added cereal to the coating mixture
- Used fat-free ice cream and fudge topping

Nutrition Scorecard *(per serving)*		
	Before	After
Calories	469	182
Fat (grams)	26	6
% calories from fat	48	25
Cholesterol (mg)	16	7

⅓ cup crisp rice cereal (such as Rice Krispies)

3 tablespoon mini chocolate chips

2 tablespoons chopped toasted pecans

4 scoops (½ cup each) fat-free vanilla ice cream

½ cup fat-free fudge topping

In a shallow bowl, toss together the cereal, chocolate chips, and pecans. Drop a scoop of ice cream into the cereal-chocolate mixture and roll quickly to coat completely, pressing the mixture into the ice cream with your fingertips. As you finish each ball, wrap it in a piece of plastic wrap and place it in the freezer. Repeat with the remaining ice cream.

To serve, spoon 2 tablespoons of the fudge topping onto 4 dessert plates or in the bottom of 4 dessert bowls. Place an ice cream ball in the center of the sauce on each plate. Serve immediately.

Cinnamon Caramel Apple Slices

Serves 4

❧❧❧❧❧

This tastes great even without heating. Just dip the raw apple slices into the spiced caramel sauce and enjoy.

How fat and calories were lowered:

▸ Reduced the amount of nuts

▸ Used a fat-free caramel topping

Nutrition Scorecard
(per serving)

	Before	After
Calories	336	188
Fat (grams)	15	4
% calories from fat	39	18
Cholesterol (mg)	11	0

4 Granny Smith apples
½ cup fat-free caramel topping

¾ teaspoon cinnamon
3 tablespoons chopped pecans

Core the apples and peel, if desired. Cut the apples into ½-inch slices. Arrange the slices in a 9-inch glass pie dish.

In a small bowl, mix together the caramel topping and cinnamon until blended. Drizzle over the apples. Sprinkle the pecans on top.

Cover the dish with microwave-safe plastic wrap. Microwave on High for 6 to 7 minutes, or until the apples are fork-tender. Check and turn once during cooking.

Serve immediately.

Chocolate Frozen Bananas

Serves 6

❈❈❈❈❈

*T**his is a fun way to use up extra bananas.*
How fat and calories were lowered:

❧ Reduced the amount of chocolate chips and replaced them in part with fat-free fudge topping

❧ Used a crisp cereal instead of nuts

❧ Eliminated the shortening

Nutrition Scorecard		
(per serving)		
	Before	*After*
Calories	568	207
Fat (grams)	42	8
% calories from fat	60	31
Cholesterol (mg)	0	0

3 large bananas, peeled

6 wooden pop sticks or wooden skewers

¾ cup semisweet chocolate chips

¼ cup fat-free fudge topping

5 teaspoons water

1¼ cups crisp rice cereal (such as Rice Krispies)

Line a tray with wax paper. Cut each banana in half crosswise. Insert a wooden stick into each banana piece and place on a tray. Freeze until firm, about 1 hour.

Combine the chocolate chips, fudge topping, and water in a microwavable bowl and microwave on High for 45 to 60 seconds. Stir until blended.

Remove the bananas from the freezer just before dipping. Dip a banana into the warm chocolate; allow excess to drip off. Immediately roll the banana in the cereal before the chocolate hardens. Repeat with the remaining bananas. Cover; return to freezer. Serve frozen.

Chocolate Raspberry Trifle

Serves 8

❈ ❈ ❈ ❈ ❈

*A*bsolutely delicious.

How fat and calories were lowered:

❧ Used nonfat milk instead of whole milk

❧ Replaced regular cake with a fat-free cake

❧ Used a light nondairy whipped topping instead of whipping cream

Nutrition Scorecard *(per serving)*		
	Before	*After*
Calories	340	218
Fat (grams)	14	2
% calories from fat	37	9
Cholesterol (mg)	154	0

12 ounces fresh raspberries

1 (3.4-ounce) package instant vanilla
    pudding mix

¾ cup nonfat milk

1¾ cups thawed frozen light nondairy
    whipped topping

1 (14-ounce) fat-free chocolate loaf cake

Wash the raspberries and remove any stems. Carefully pat dry with paper towels and set aside.

In a medium bowl, combine the pudding mix with the milk. Whisk 1½ to 2 minutes, or until thickened. Fold the thawed whipped topping into the pudding until well blended.

Cut the loaf cake crosswise into ½-inch-thick slices.

To assemble the trifle, arrange 4 or 5 of the cake slices in a 2-quart glass serving bowl to cover the bottom of the dish. Spread half the pudding mixture over the cake. Distribute half the raspberries evenly over the pudding. Repeat these layers, using the remaining cake slices, pudding mixture, and raspberries. Serve immediately or cover and refrigerate until serving time.

Cake Bowl Lime Dip with Fresh Fruit

Serves 8

✄ ✄ ✄ ✄ ✄

Such a spectacular way to serve a fruit dip—*in a hollowed-out cake.*
How fat and calories were lowered:

☛ Used a fat-free loaf cake instead of pound cake

☛ Substituted nonfat yogurt for cream cheese

☛ Reduced the amount of sugar

Nutrition Scorecard *(per serving)*		
	Before	*After*
Calories	405	203
Fat *(grams)*	21	0
% calories from fat	44	1
Cholesterol *(mg)*	156	1

2 cups strawberries

1 (14-ounce) fat-free golden loaf cake

8 ounces plain nonfat yogurt

3 tablespoons honey

3 tablespoons powdered sugar

2 tablespoons fresh lime juice

2 teaspoons finely grated lime zest

Wash and hull the strawberries and pat dry with paper towels; set aside.

Cutting from the top of the loaf cake, hollow out the loaf, leaving a ½-inch-thick shell. Cut the cake removed from the center into cubes; set aside.

In a small bowl, combine the yogurt, honey, powdered sugar, lime juice, and lime zest. Transfer the dip into the center of the cake. Serve immediately.

To serve, give each person a plate of cake cubes and strawberries to dip into the yogurt mixture.

Angel Food Cake Bowl Lime Dip with Fresh Fruit

Follow the same procedure as above, but substitute a commercial angel food cake for the loaf cake. Slice the top off the cake and hollow out a trench.

Aunt Mickey's Strawberry Pineapple Gelatin

Serves 8

⨳⨳ ⨳⨳ ⨳⨳

W*hen I was a kid, I would do anything to get an extra piece of my Aunt Mickey's gelatin dessert—even wash the dishes. To this day I still don't like washing dishes, but I still love her dessert. I've made many versions of this favorite recipe, and I think this one is the best yet. Tip: To get a head start, chill the crushed pineapple.*

How fat and calories were lowered:

- Used fat-free cream cheese and fat-free sour cream instead of their regular counterparts

- Reduced the amount of sugar

- Used a sugar-free gelatin

Nutrition Scorecard
(per serving)

	Before	After
Calories	309	166
Fat (grams)	13	0
% calories from fat	38	0
Cholesterol (mg)	37	5

1½ cups boiling water

1 (0.6-ounce) package sugar-free raspberry gelatin

2 (10-ounce) packages frozen sliced strawberries, partially thawed

1 (20-ounce) can crushed pineapple (juice-packed), drained

8 ounces fat-free cream cheese, at room temperature

3 tablespoons sugar

½ cup fat-free sour cream

In a large bowl, stir together the water and gelatin until the gelatin is dissolved. Stir in the strawberries and pineapple. Pour half the mixture into an 8-inch square pan. Chill in the refrigerator while making the filling.

Set the remaining gelatin mixture aside at room temperature.

Meanwhile, beat together the cream cheese and sugar in a small bowl. Fold in the sour cream. Carefully spread the cheese mixture on top of the semifirm gelatin. Then spoon the remaining gelatin mixture over the top. Chill until firm. Cut into pieces to serve.

Tropical Ambrosia (Fat-Free, Too)

Serves 8

⨯⨯ ⨯⨯ ⨯⨯ ⨯⨯ ⨯⨯

This is a family favorite that can be made year-round. I used to make this dish with shredded coconut but discovered that a potent splash of coconut extract works surprisingly well.

How fat and calories were lowered:

☞ Used fruits packed in fruit juice

☞ Replaced coconut with coconut extract

☞ Used fat-free sour cream instead of regular sour cream

Nutrition Scorecard
(per serving)

	Before	After
Calories	279	138
Fat (grams)	13	0
% calories from fat	40	0
Cholesterol (mg)	13	0

3 cups miniature marshmallows

1 (8-ounce) can crushed pineapple (juice-packed), drained

1 (20-ounce) can pineapple chunks (juice-packed), drained

1 (11-ounce) can water-packed mandarin oranges, drained

1 cup fat-free sour cream

1 teaspoon coconut extract

In a large bowl, combine the marshmallows, crushed pineapple, pineapple chunks, and mandarin oranges. In a small bowl, combine the sour cream and coconut extract. Gently fold the sour cream mixture into the marshmallow mixture and fold until blended.

Apricot Coconut Chews

Makes 24 pieces

✥✥✥✥✥

Th**ese little jewels make a great snack.**
How fat and calories were lowered:

☛ Used less flaked coconut and added oats

☛ Used less chocolate chips

☛ Used fat-free sweetened condensed milk

Nutrition Scorecard
(per piece)

	Before	After
Calories	102	89
Fat (grams)	5	3
% calories from fat	39	30
Cholesterol (mg)	5	2

7-ounces dried apricots

1½ cups flaked coconut

½ cup quick oats

½ cup fat-free sweetened condensed milk

⅓ cup miniature chocolate chips

¼ cup powdered sugar

Finely chop the apricots in a food processor. In a medium bowl, combine the chopped apricots, coconut, and oats. Mix well. Stir in the sweetened condensed milk. Add the chocolate chips and blend.

Using the palms of your hands, roll small amounts of the mixture into 1¼-inch balls. Roll the balls in powdered sugar and place on waxed paper. Serve immediately, or cover and refrigerate.

Strawberry Layer Cake (Fat-Free, Too)

Serves 9

✷ ✷ ✷ ✷

Such a beautiful way to show off and enjoy strawberries.
How fat and calories were lowered:

☛ Replaced buttercream frosting with nonfat vanilla pudding

☛ Used a fat-free commercial cake

Nutrition Scorecard		
(per serving)		
	Before	*After*
Calories	514	222
Fat (grams)	34	0
% calories from fat	59	0
Cholesterol (mg)	193	0

1 (14-ounce) fat-free golden loaf cake

2 pints strawberries

Strawberry Filling

¼ cup powdered sugar

2 tablespoons strawberry jam

1 tablespoon fresh lemon juice

Vanilla Filling

1 (3.4-ounce) package instant vanilla
    pudding

1 cup nonfat milk

Slice the crown off of the top of the cake (about ¼ inch thick) and reserve. Cut the cake horizontally into 6 long slices (about ½ inch thick) and set aside. Wash and hull strawberries and dry well on paper towels. Reserve 12 to 15 large berries for garnish; slice remaining strawberries thinly (to equal about 2 cups) for use in the filling.

To make the strawberry filling: In a medium bowl, stir together the powdered sugar, jam, and lemon juice. Add the sliced strawberries and toss gently. Let stand for 30 minutes.

To make the vanilla filling: In a medium bowl, whisk together the pudding mix and milk for 1 to 2 minutes, until thickened.

To assemble the cake: Place 2 cake slices side by side in an 8-inch square pan, to form a square. Use parts of the "crown" to fill in any gaps. Spread one-third of the vanilla filling over the cake slices. Top with half of the strawberry filling. Repeat (2 cake slices, one-third vanilla filling, and remaining strawberry filling). Top with the remaining cake layer and the remaining vanilla filling. Cut the reserved whole strawberries in half lengthwise. Arrange decoratively over the top of the vanilla filling, cut sides down.

Chocolate Butterscotch Haystacks

Makes 42

✄ ✄ ✄ ✄ ✄

This candylike treat was a childhood favorite. How fat and calories were lowered:

🖎 Used fat-free sweetened condensed milk

🖎 Used less butterscotch chips

🖎 Replaced almonds with crisp rice cereal

Nutrition Scorecard *(per serving)*		
	Before	After
Calories	110	76
Fat (grams)	6	3
% calories from fat	52	34
Cholesterol (mg)	3	0

4 ounces semisweet cooking chocolate, broken into pieces

¾ cup butterscotch chips

1 (14-ounce) can fat-free sweetened condensed milk

1½ cups crisp rice cereal (such as Rice Krispies)

3 cups chow mein noodles

Line two baking sheets with wax paper. In a large saucepan, combine the chocolate, butterscotch chips, and sweetened condensed milk and cook, over low heat, stirring constantly, until chocolate is melted and mixture is smooth. Remove from the heat. Add the rice cereal and noodles and mix lightly. Using two forks, drop candy in small clusters onto prepared cookie sheets. Chill until firm. Store covered in a cool, dry place.

Fresh Strawberry Pie

Serves 6

❈ ❈ ❈ ❈ ❈

This is the easiest pie I ever made, yet it looks like one of those you'll find in pie shops during the peak of the strawberry season.

How fat and calories were lowered:

☞ Used a commercial reduced-fat graham cracker crust

☞ Used a low-sugar jam instead of prepared glaze

☞ Replaced whipping cream with a scoop of fat-free vanilla ice cream

Nutrition Scorecard *(per serving)*		
	Before	After
Calories	531	360
Fat (grams)	30	5
% calories from fat	49	11
Cholesterol (mg)	54	0

3 pints fresh strawberries, chilled

½ cup strawberry jam

1 commercial 9-inch reduced-fat graham cracker crust

6 scoops (½ cup each) fat-free vanilla ice cream (optional)

Rinse, dry, and hull the strawberries. Set aside half of the strawberries, choosing the nicest-looking ones to remain whole. Slice the remaining berries.

Microwave the jam on High until melted (about 15 seconds). Spoon a thin layer of the jam over the bottom of the pie crust. Place all the sliced berries evenly in the pie shell and top with about half the jam.

Arrange the whole berries on top (pointed end up), piling them up in the center. Spoon the remaining jam over the whole berries and in between. Refrigerate until the jam is set. Serve with a scoop of fat-free vanilla ice cream, if desired.

Desserts Categorized by Fat

Virtually Fat-Free
(0 to 0.5 grams fat)

Almost Fat-Free Cheesecake

Angel Food Cake Bowl Lime Dip with Fresh Fruit

Aunt Mickey's Strawberry Pineapple Gelatin

Blueberry Pie

Boysenberry Sour Cream Crumb

Cake Bowl Lime Dip with Fresh Fruit

Cool Lemon Slush

Cranberry Citrus Bundt Bread (Fat-Free, Too)

Dried-Cherry Muffins

Fat-Free Apple Turnovers

Fat-Free Apricot Fool

Fat-Free Phyllo Crust

Fresh Strawberry Shake

Glazed Poppy Seed Bread

Orange Cream Cheese Bavarian

Orange Essence Prune Whip

Peachy Cheesecake

Pear-Apple Pie

Raspberry Dapple Muffins

Strawberry Layer Cake (Fat-Free)

Sweet Potato Bread

Tropical Ambrosia (Fat-Free)

Tropical Shake

Vanilla Bean Pudding

Zesty Lemon Sherbet

Desserts Containing 1 to 3 Fat Grams

Amaretto Chocolate Pudding

Apple Streusel Muffins

Apricot Coconut Chews

Apricot Oat Bars

Blueberry Buckle Bread

Boston Cream Pie

Buttermilk Spice "Doughnuts"

Butterscotch Chip Cookies

Cheesecake Brownies

Chewy Fruity Molasses Bars

Chocolate Butterscotch Haystacks

Chocolate Chip Almond Coconut Cookies

Chocolate Cookie Crust

Chocolate Meringue Cookies

Chocolate Raspberry Trifle

Chocolate Tapioca

Cinnayum Cookies

Crispy Almond Lace Cookies

Crispy Orange Lace Cookies

Easy Mini Cheesecakes

Easy Truffles

Frozen Raspberry Ribbon Pie

Jam Thumbprint Cookies

Key Lime Pie

Lemon Bars

Maple-Frosted "Doughnuts"

Mile-High Sundae Pie

Mississippi Mud Muffins

Molasses Chews

Oatmeal Pecan Cookies

Oatmeal Raisin Cookies

Orange Date Bars

Peanut Butter Chip Brownies

Peanut Butter Cookies

Pineapple Upside-Down Cake

Pumpkin Bars

Rocky Road Fudge Surprise

Sweet Potato Pudding

Desserts Containing 4 to 6 Fat Grams

Almond Amaretto Cheesecake

Apple Crisp

Black Forest Brownies

Cappuccino Raspberry Cake

Carrot Spice Cake

Cherry Crunch

Cherry Delicious

Chocolate Bread Pudding

Chocolate Chip Muffins

Chocolate Crunch Ice Cream Balls

Chocolate Fudge Pudding

Chocolate Turtle Pecan Cookies

Cinnamon Caramel Apple Slices

Cinnamon Streusel Coffee Cake

Cranberry Orange Cheesecake

Crispy Nutty Bars

Double Chocolate Chip Brownies

Easy Chocolate Mousse

Easy Mocha Mousse

Five-Layer Bars

Fresh Strawberry Pie

Giant Carrot-Apple Muffins

Glazed Lemon Nut Bread

Grasshopper Mint Pie

Hawaiian Mandarin Cake

Hazelnut Mousse

Hazelnut Torte Roll

Lemon Cheesecake

Lemon Intensity Bundt Cake

Lemon Meringue Pie

Lime Daiquiri Cheesecake

Macaroon Brownies

Mint Chocolate Marble Cheesecake

Nancy's Eclairs

Orange Sunshine Cake

Peach Melba Tart

Peach Pecan Crumb Muffins

Peanut Butter Ice Cream Squares

Pecan Bars

Piña Colada Cheesecake

Pumpkin Cheesecake

Pumpkin Pudding Cake

Raspberry Cheesecake

Raspberry Thrill Pie

Red-White-and-Blueberry Mold

Sweet Potato Pie

Three-Layer Fudge Bars

Tropical Macadamia Nut Bread

Very Blueberry Swirl Cheesecake

Wendy's Cookies

White Chocolate Mousse with Raspberry
  Compote

Desserts Containing 7 to 10 Fat Grams

Caramel Pecan Ice Cream Pie

Chocolate Frozen Bananas

Chocolate Zucchini Snack Cake

Crème Brûlée

Easy Tiramisù

Fluffy Mocha Pie

Frozen Peanut Butter Fudge Pie

Fudgy Blackbottom Pie

Maple Pecan Coffee Cake

Pecan Caramel Cheesecake

Rainbow Freeze

Strawberry Surprise Cheesecake

Strawberry Yogurt Pie

Triple Chocolate Cheesecake

Desserts Categorized by Calories

Desserts Containing 100 Calories or Less

Apricot Coconut Chews
Apricot Oat Bars
Butterscotch Chip Cookies
Chocolate Butterscotch Haystacks
Chocolate Chip Almond Coconut Cookies
Chocolate Cookie Crust
Chocolate Meringue Cookies
Chocolate Turtle Pecan Cookies
Cinnayum Cookies
Crispy Almond Lace Cookies
Crispy Orange Lace Cookies
Easy Truffles
Fat-Free Phyllo Crust
Jam Thumbprint Cookies
Lemon Bars
Molasses Chews
Oatmeal Pecan Cookies
Oatmeal Raisin Cookies
Orange Date Bars
Peanut Butter Cookies
Pumpkin Bars
Rocky Road Fudge Surprise

Desserts Containing 101 to 150 Calories

Buttermilk Spice "Doughnuts"
Chewy Fruity Molasses Bars
Double Chocolate Chip Brownies
Easy Mini Cheesecakes
Fat-Free Apple Turnovers
Five-Layer Bars
Glazed Poppy Seed Bread
Macaroon Brownies
Maple-Frosted "Doughnuts"
Mississippi Mud Muffins
One-Crust Pastry
Orange Cream Cheese Bavarian
Orange Essence Prune Whip
Peanut Butter Chip Brownies
Pecan Bars
Three-Layer Fudge Bars
Tropical Ambrosia (Fat-Free)
Wendy's Cookies

Desserts Containing 151 to 200 Calories

Almost Fat-Free Cheesecake

Aunt Mickey's Strawberry Pineapple Gelatin

Blueberry Pie

Cheesecake Brownies

Chocolate Crunch Ice Cream Balls

Chocolate Fudge Pudding

Chocolate Tapioca

Cinnamon Caramel Apple Slices

Cool Lemon Slush

Cranberry Citrus Bundt Bread (Fat-Free, Too)

Crème Brûlée

Crispy Nutty Bars

Glazed Lemon Nut Bread

Hazelnut Torte Roll

Nancy's Eclairs

Peach Melba Tart

Peanut Butter Ice Cream Squares

Raspberry Cheesecake

Red-White-and-Blueberry Mold

Sweet Potato Bread

Vanilla Bean Pudding

Zesty Lemon Sherbet

Desserts Containing 201 to 250 Calories

Almond Amaretto Cheesecake

Amaretto Chocolate Pudding

Angel Food Cake Bowl Lime Dip with Fresh Fruit

Blueberry Buckle Bread

Boysenberry Sour Cream Crumb

Cake Bowl Lime Dip with Fresh Fruit

Chocolate Frozen Bananas

Chocolate Raspberry Trifle

Cranberry Orange Cheesecake

Easy Tiramisù

Fat-Free Apricot Fool

Fluffy Mocha Pie

Lemon Cheesecake

Lime Daiquiri Cheesecake

Mint Chocolate Marble Cheesecake

Peachy Cheesecake

Pear Apple Pie

Pecan Caramel Cheesecake

Pineapple Upside-Down Cake

Piña Colada Cheesecake

Pumpkin Pudding Cake

Rainbow Freeze

Raspberry Dapple Muffins

Raspberry Thrill Pie

Strawberry Layer Cake (Fat-Free)

Sweet Potato Pudding

Triple Chocolate Cheesecake

Tropical Macadamia Nut Bread

Very Blueberry Swirl Cheesecake

Desserts Containing 251 to 300 Calories

Black Forest Brownies

Boston Cream Pie

Carrot Spice Cake

Cherry Crunch

Cherry Delicious

Chocolate Zucchini Snack Cake

Easy Chocolate Mousse

Easy Mocha Mousse

Fresh Strawberry Shake

Grasshopper Mint Pie

Hawaiian Mandarin Cake

Hazelnut Mousse

Key Lime Pie

Lemon Intensity Bundt Cake

Lemon Meringue Pie

Maple Pecan Coffee Cake

Orange Sunshine Cake

Pumpkin Cheesecake

Strawberry Surprise Cheesecake

Strawberry Yogurt Pie

Sweet Potato Pie

Tropical Shake

White Chocolate Mousse with Raspberry
    Compote

Cinnamon Streusel Coffee Cake

Dried-Cherry Muffins

Frozen Peanut Butter Fudge Pie

Frozen Raspberry Ribbon Pie

Fudgy Blackbottom Pie

No-Bake Peanut Butter Cheese Pie

Peach Pecan Crumb Muffins

Desserts Containing 301 to 350 Calories

Apple Crisp

Cappuccino Raspberry Cake

Chocolate Bread Pudding

Chocolate Chip Muffins

Index

Substitutions

Zoom in on high-fat ingredients in your favorite recipe. Then try to replace them with ingredients lower in fat. Just changing one ingredient in a recipe can make a substantial difference. Here are some of my favorite substitutions.

Amount	Instead of	Substitute	Calories saved	Fat saved (grams)
1 cup	almonds, chopped	½ cup chopped almonds + ½ cup crisp rice cereal	327	34
1 cup	almonds, chopped	1 cup *sliced* almonds	212	19
½ cup	butter	½ cup light butter	406	46
½ cup	butter (for baking)	½ cup unsweetened applesauce	808	92
½ cup	butter (for baking)	½ cup baby-food prunes	681	92
½ cup	butter (for frosting)	½ cup marshmallow creme	392	92
2 ounces	chocolate, baking	⅓ cup unsweetened cocoa powder	215	25
1 cup	chocolate chips	½ cup mini chocolate chips	300	29
8 ounces	cream cheese	8 ounces light tub-style cream cheese	305	38
8 ounces	cream cheese	8 ounces light brick cream cheese	200	25
8 ounces	cream cheese	8 ounces fat-free (tub-style or brick-style) cream cheese	588	79
8 ounces	cream cheese	1 cup nonfat cottage cheese, pureed	651	79
1	egg, whole	2 egg whites	41	5
1 cup	heavy cream	1 cup evaporated skim milk	621	87
8 ounces	mascarpone cheese	4 ounces mascarpone + 4 ounces fat-free ricotta	467	58
½ cup	oil (for baking)	½ cup unsweetened applesauce	911	109
½ cup	oil (for baking)	½ cup baby-food prunes	832	109
1 cup	peanut butter	1 cup reduced-fat peanut butter	0	32
1 cup	sour cream	1 cup fat-free sour cream	340	47
1 cup	sour cream	1 cup nonfat plain yogurt	360	47
1 cup	sweetened condensed milk	fat-free sweetened condensed milk	102	27
1 cup	whipped cream	1 cup nondairy light whipped topping	256	35
1 cup	whole milk	1 cup nonfat milk	64	8
1 cup	whole milk	1 cup buttermilk (for baking)	51	6